American Houses

American

Houses

Philip Langdon

Stewart, Tabori & Chang
New York

For Maryann

Text copyright © 1987 by Philip Langdon
Photo credits begin on page 249

The publisher is grateful for permission to quote
from the song "Little Boxes"
Words and music by Malvina Reynolds
Used by permission. All rights reserved.

Portions of this book originally appeared
in a different form in *The Atlantic.*

Published in 1987 by Stewart, Tabori & Chang, Inc.
740 Broadway, New York, New York 10003

Library of Congress Cataloging-in-Publication Data

Langdon, Philip.
  American houses.

Bibliography: p.
  Includes index.
    1. Architecture, Domestic — United States.
  2. Dwellings — United States — History — 20th century.
  I. Title.
  NA7205.L35   1987   728′.0973   86-23158
  ISBN 0-941434-96-6

Distributed by Workman Publishing
1 West 39 Street, New York, New York 10018

Printed in Japan

10 9 8 7 6 5 4 3 2 1

Design: J. C. Suarès
         Diana M. Jones

Contents

Preface

PRECEDING PAGES
Call it Craftsman Revival or 1920s bungalow turned crisply contemporary—this Omaha house by Daniel Solomon and John Goldman clearly expresses the current fascination with a basic American house-form: center door, symmetrical windows, and a sociable porch all under the broad slopes of a sheltering roof, squarely facing the street.

This book is the result of thousands of miles of travel throughout the United States, examining the latest in American houses. My first real immersion in the striking variety and rapidly changing character of America's houses came when William Whitworth, editor of *The Atlantic* and a man fascinated with just about every aspect of residential design and construction, commissioned me to take a close look at today's houses—an assignment that lasted months and took me from post-and-beam houses in York Harbor, Maine, to factory-built houses in rural Maryland, to magnificently crafted houses in Atlanta, to solar and earth-sheltered dwellings in Davis, California, to condominiums built on top of office buildings in downtown San Francisco.

I had been writing for a decade about housing, real estate, and design, but it was my journeys for *The Atlantic* that sharpened my appreciation of the imagination and creativity being infused into what we Americans call home. The 15,000-word article I wrote was published in September 1984. It later won the National Association of Home Builders Golden Hammer Award as the year's best magazine article on housing, as well as a citation for *The Atlantic* from the American Institute of Architects for excellent coverage of architecture. The piece was distributed by American embassies overseas and was even translated into Chinese for distribution in the People's Republic of China. An auspicious beginning—but, happily, only a beginning.

Andrew Stewart—president of Stewart, Tabori & Chang, which had earned a reputation for publishing beautifully illustrated books—then came to me with a proposal: that I continue my travels, expand their scope, and produce a book-length look at today's American houses. Regions and subjects that were passed over or touched on only lightly in the magazine article could now be explored at length. Most of the book would focus on recently constructed houses—from one-of-a-kind architect-designed homes to houses created by major homebuilding companies to vast and ambitious new complexes like Bertrand Goldberg's River City in Chicago. But *American Houses* would also assess one of the most notable phenomena of the past two decades—the rapid growth of restoration, renovation, and rehabilitation of old houses and the conversion of all sorts of other buildings to residential use.

In architecture and design, there is still no substitute for first-hand examination. In 1985–1986, I traveled from Lowell, Massachusetts, to Sarasota to San Antonio to Seattle and to dozens of points in between, visiting oceanfront resort homes, modest but surprisingly generous-feeling starter homes, factories and schools that had been turned into high-ceilinged apartments, and countless other kinds of houses; the great majority of houses and developments I discuss in the text are places I actually visited. Along the way, I also talked to architects, builders, designers, developers, academics, planners, craftsmen, and a good many owners and occupants about this diverse collection of houses. My hope is that readers—whether they're people working in the housing field or homeowners thinking about what they want in their next house—will get from this book a heightened understanding of today's American houses and how they're changing. This book attempts to show what's new in American houses, what innovations are worth looking at, and, in some cases, what should be avoided. From among the many innovations and advances presented in *American Houses,* I hope readers will find ideas they will be able to use in the future.

Introduction

OPPOSITE, CLOCKWISE FROM TOP LEFT
Rose-covered walkways at Charleston Place in Boca del Mar, Florida, reintroduce suburbanites to the pleasures of intimately-scaled public spaces. Donald MacDonald's upward-thrusting "snowflake house" strikes an invigorating contrast against its hillside setting. Condos at Golden Gateway Commons achieve a gardenlike atmosphere on top of a San Francisco office building. A Modernist house by Julian and Barbara Neski floats serenely above the bushy Long Island landscape, framing views in all directions.

P eople carry in their minds a picture of what constitutes an "American house." For most of us, it is and has long been a freestanding dwelling that rises from its own piece of land. Whether that piece of land is a 40-foot-wide lot on a city street or an expanse of farmland stretching off toward the horizon is almost irrelevant; what matters is that the house stands as an individual object, separate from the walls of neighbors. This may not be the sort of dwelling in which every American actually lives—millions inhabit apartment buildings and blocks of row houses—yet the detached house holds such allure for the imagination that it remains a national ideal, in good times and bad, in periods both of dense urban development and of outward suburban dispersal. So deeply embedded in the country's consciousness is the ideal of a freestanding dwelling that even young children, when asked to draw a house, will unhesitatingly make a sketch of a family-sized dwelling with a pitched roof on top, a few windows in its façade, and a prominent front door.

Some of the details that embellish this notion of the American house have, of course, changed greatly with the passage of time. In the 1850s, when the landscape architect Andrew Jackson Downing was exerting a major influence on residential design, the image of an American house would have included verandas and vestibules, parlors and pantries. In the 1920s, a decade enchanted by "Old English" architecture but also gripped by a concern for cleanliness, it often summoned up a picturesque, even quaint, exterior with arched doorways and a steeply pitched roof, yet with a shiny white-surfaced kitchen and bathroom within. In the 1960s, the prevailing vision was of a house that had substituted a back patio or deck for the front porch and had added a "family room" as a casual, unceremonious alternative to the formality of the living room.

Despite such modifications, the governing ideal remained constant in its essentials—an individual residence enclosing a comfortable amount of space beneath the slopes of its roof and enjoying dominion over a certain amount of land beyond its walls. Gradually, too, the American house was accompanied by a standard arrangement of its grounds: in the front grew a neatly kept lawn, setting a scene that possessed a measure of dignity and repose. To the rear, a more informal yard provided a place for relaxation and outdoor recreation. Side yards acted as buffers against the noise and nosiness of neighbors, while at the same time making each household feel more autonomous.

This was by no means a perfect or universal way to provide shelter, but it did satisfy many of the needs of millions of people. From East Coast to West, vast numbers of houses were built in accordance with the common image of an American house—dwellings set apart from one another in a pattern that suited, above all, the interests of families.

Today much of this arrangement has lost its most important reason for being: the traditional family—a working husband, a wife who stays home, and their not-yet-grown children—until recently the predominant form of American household, now makes up a minority of America's population. As the composition of the household and the work force has dramatically changed, the house has been pressed to adapt. Detached dwellings accounted for 80 percent of the newly constructed private housing in the United States as late as 1975; a decade later, the proportion had steadily diminished to 62 percent. Instead of an "American house," it's becoming more accurate to speak in the plural: "American houses." The nation has entered a period in which many houses are distinguished less by their lingering similarities than by how they diverge both from one another and from homes of the past.

The trend toward more varied forms of housing holds contrasting meanings for different people; it can be likened to the mixture of motivations that sent explorers and settlers into the undeveloped reaches of North America before the twentieth century. Just as some people confidently opened up a new geographic domain in a quest for a better life, today there are some who launch into new architectural territory, searching for housing superior to the typical dwellings of the past. A few, like contemporary Lewises and Clarks, explore risky and breathtaking terrain, far ahead of any mass migration. A great many more, by contrast, resemble the pioneers who were driven onward by necessity; like those who pushed westward because they couldn't find opportunity in their native regions, many today are moving to innovative housing simply because the old standard of a detached house has slipped out of their financial grasp. The varied forms of today's houses do not spring from a single impulse; the motivations are as disparate as the houses themselves.

If some of America's newest houses are deliberately earth-shaking, certainly most are not. The alteration of home design, planning, and construction is a cautious endeavor, careful not to go too far too fast. This pragmatic style of change—subject to continuous reconsideration of whether to push farther on or make a discreet retreat—fits the American penchant for treating a house as a product that must later be resold, and at a profit. Few are willing to be burdened with a house that will be difficult to pass on to another, yet-unknown purchaser. Even when designers and builders entertain radical ideas, they have to overcome the con-

servatism of financiers and the wariness of homebuyers who view a house not as a permanent family seat but as a commodity to be turned over quickly at some future date. Flights of fancy are considered chancy.

So there are deep-rooted reasons for houses to hew closely to tradition, and revolutionary design is rare. In the air today is practically none of the flashy 1950s-style futurism—the expectation that American houses will soon be transformed into push-button domiciles equipped with such amenities as private helicopter pads. (That was a flight of fancy that never took off.) Yet customary approaches to housing are nonetheless being challenged—if not by conventional builders, then by a few daring individuals and organizations, if not in every tract development, then in houses and projects scattered throughout the United States. Routine ways survive, but anyone who investigates thoroughly will find that innovation is being demanded—and is appearing—in nearly every significant aspect of American houses: their location, connection to the surrounding community, construction, esthetics, use of energy, sensitivity to climate, adaptability to work and leisure, and capacity for accommodating different kinds of households.

Society has changed too much for houses to remain pervaded by yesterday's customs. Millions of people who are divorced, widowed, or single now live alone, and they're wielding a growing influence on home design. Until about a decade ago, unattached individuals, especially those who had never married, were often rele-

OVERLEAF
William F. Stern's Wroxton Street houses confer a unifying rhythm on a suburban street near Houston. They also suggest that one way of coping with cars is to cede ground floor to vehicles and let people take their Postmodern pleasures at second-story level.

Like the wagons of pioneers, houses at Sun City gathered in circles—but permanently and on a grand scale.

gated to rental apartments, but today they increasingly buy their residences—and, as owners, they can impel builders and designers to pay closer attention to their tastes and requirements. Childless couples have proliferated. So have single-parent families. So have people of retirement age and other households who differ in some respect from the traditional nuclear family. As a result, changes are beginning to be generated in the country's housing, and an increasing diversity in the years ahead seems likely. We're beyond the point of pretending that one or two or three forms of housing will fit everyone's needs. A broad terrain situated between the single-family home and the nursing home is starting to be staked out. This book brings together many of the fresh ideas that are being developed.

If you were to try to establish when and where the seeds of today's more varied housing took root, one place you would have to look to is southern Arizona in 1959. There, a sixty-year-old builder, Delbert Eugene Webb, announced that he was going to put golf courses, swimming pools, community centers, and a vast number of one-story houses on the flat desert

30 miles northwest of Phoenix, enticing thousands of retirees to settle on land that until then had been irrigated fields of cotton. Nobody had ever undertaken a venture quite like Webb's—the development of a sizable town inhabited solely by older people and furnished with an array of community facilities even before the first house was offered for sale.

Webb—a one-time semiprofessional baseball player who established a construction company in Phoenix in the 1920s and did well enough that, by 1945, he was able to buy a part-interest in the New York Yankees—conducted a careful study before deciding to embark on his visionary project. His Del E. Webb Development Company sought advice from business consultants, psychiatrists, and older people themselves. His executives looked especially closely at a small Arizona development called Youngtown, where, since 1954, more than 100 houses —modest dwellings with few public amenities other than a water-storage lake—had been purchased by people of retirement age. Finally, Webb's corporation went ahead, acquiring the rights to 20,000 acres and committing itself to spending $1.3 million to start the new town. Webb named it Sun City.

When it became clear to observers that this unusual development was not a grandiose illusion—that an astonishing 262 houses had been sold on the first weekend and that, by the end of 1962, more than 1,300 houses would be contracted for—Webb captured national attention, his wary-eyed, tight-lipped face appearing on the cover of *Time,* with a shuffleboard court in the background. The shuffleboard court was an inevitable symbol: a half-dozen shuffleboard courts had been installed before opening day, and, by 1980, Sun City would boast seventy-two of them. But they were part of what was conceived from the start as an extraordinarily comprehensive recreation and activity program. Although Webb died in 1974, his company continued to flourish. By 1980, it had supplied Sun City with 5 auditoriums, 7 swimming pools, 8 lawn-bowling greens, 11 golf courses, 17 tennis courts, 40 bowling lanes, and numerous other community facilities.

Today, Sun City is an orderly expanse of 26,000 homes with cactus growing on the gravelly front yards and replicas of roadrunners decorating more than a few of the garage doors. It claims a population of 46,000 senior citizens (average age sixty-nine), many of whom travel the immaculate streets on golf carts outfitted with windshields. Since 1978, the Del E. Webb Development Company has been constructing an extension nearby—Sun City West, whose population has passed 13,000—and, in 1986, the company started building Sun City Vistoso, northwest of Tucson. The company also established smaller Sun Cities near Riverside, California, and on Florida's Gulf Coast.

Other developers observed Webb's success and decided to embark on similar ventures. Southeastern Florida became the site of four Century Villages—retirement communities appealing especially to Jewish migrants from the urban Northeast. As many as 17,000 people live behind the continually guarded gates of a single complex. Like Sun Cities, each Century Village provides its residents with places to swim, bike, or dance, to play tennis or shuffleboard or pinochle, to sew, paint, take in shows, enroll in classes, or enjoy other activities.

Neither Webb's company nor Cenvill Development Corporation, the organizer of Century Villages, designed its housing to be radically different from what was being built for other segments of the population. Promoting the idea of a separate society for the retired and implementing it, with all the services it implied, was a substantial challenge in itself. The housing approximated what the occupants had already been accustomed to. From 1960 to the present, most Sun City homes have been detached two-bedroom dwellings—a little smaller but not terribly different from what their owners had left behind in Kansas City or Minneapolis, except that the sunniest part of the house is designated the "Arizona room." Century Villages contain dozens of three- and four-story apartment buildings—familiar enough to city dwellers from New York or Philadelphia—with landscaped grounds between the buildings to make the setting more relaxed. The retirement housing of a Sun City or a Century Village differs from other housing chiefly in its details: deep drawers rather than standard base cabinets to make kitchen storage more accessible, grab bars in the bathrooms, buttons for summoning help in an emergency, and no changes of level.

Since the New Year's Day grand opening in 1960, when cars containing hundreds of older people first clogged the highway into Sun City, many retirement communities have entered a second phase, one in which fundamental changes in the design of the housing are keys to the development's appeal; some of the alternatives now being developed in housing for older people are examined in Chapter Two. The important point here is that the field of retirement housing has set one of the boldest precedents of the past thirty years, demonstrating the potential for houses or developments that are aimed at well-defined segments of the population. Through the huge success of the original Sun City, Del Webb ultimately concentrated the housing industry's—and the nation's—attention on the potential for communities of the like-minded—buildings, subdivisions, compounds, and communities tailored to age bracket, interests, or other attributes of a specific group. It is

this idea from which many contemporary design innovations spring.

Seen from this perspective, the "swinging singles" complexes that attracted so much gossip a few years later are an elaboration on the Sun City concept—the clustering together of people of similar ages or outlooks. For singles in search of sociability, housing has often consisted of small apartments built close together near a pool, clubhouse, or other gathering place. The same phenomenon is evident in "empty-nester" condominiums, which became prominent throughout the country in the 1970s. Their distinctive features—outdoor space maintained by an owners' association, a sizable living-and-dining area, fewer bedrooms than in a detached house, and a relatively high quality of finish—

Strong, simple forms, in some instances with classical overtones, lend power to the house of Texas limestone that Hal Box designed for his family in Austin (above), and to a Houston house designed with richly layered effects by Fisher-Friedman Associates.

suit the needs and tastes of couples whose children are now on their own. Chapter Two, then, inspects various approaches to designing houses for single people, couples, families with children at home, adults who work at home, and those who want homes shaped by other conditions—from a desire for bright, sociable kitchens to a yearning for a private retreat.

Equally relevant to the character of a house is its setting. Chapter One focuses on a broad assortment of settings, from spectacular oceanside vantage points to grassy suburban locations to urban sites that were previously bypassed because of noise and congestion. Economic pressures are spurring residential development on unusual sites and at higher densities; in the process, they are testing the creativity of architects. In fact, because of the complexity of this challenge, architects are exerting a growing influence over the meshing of house and land. Even in regions with extraordinarily high real estate costs, where detached houses have to make do with tiny lots, it's possible, with careful design, to supply households with enjoyable private outdoor areas. In complexes of dozens of attached units, the buildings can be designed around an oasislike central landscape. Whether at ground level or at rooftop height, designers are finding ingenious ways to capitalize on a setting's potential.

At the same time, architects, builders, and occupants are giving much closer scrutiny to the house's relationship to its climate. Ever since the first oil embargo, in 1973, energy has been a key homebuilding issue. This hasn't always brought pleasing results. Chapter Three looks in part at the peculiar first legacy of the energy scare of 1973–1974—a spate of ungainly-looking solar houses and of technology that worked better in theory than in practice. Fortunately, there is more to the story: the single-mindedness of solar architecture eventually began to be tempered by a concern for other factors that contribute just as significantly to a building's success or failure; gradually the technology became more dependable, less exotic. Saving energy evolved into a more balanced endeavor. Residential construction methods have been permanently altered by the energy scares of the 1970s.

Some of the most interesting residential work now taking place, however, is not the construction of brand-new houses. It's the restoration or rehabilitation of run-down old houses and the conversion of warehouses, churches, schools, and factories to living quarters. The revival of a kaleidoscopic assortment of old buildings—a movement that, incidentally, illustrates the futility of trying to identify a house that's "typical" of our times—has blossomed in the past decade and a half into a national phenomenon. The growing affinity for old, often urban, buildings with disparate original functions represents, in many cases, the spurning of conventional suburban houses; in more than a few minds, the conventional house of a few years back has been found lacking in craftsmanship, historic character, and proximity to city stimulation. The interconnected issues of interest in old buildings and of concern for construction and craftsmanship loom large; they are explored at length in Chapter Four, which examines how (and how well or how poorly) new houses are built, and Chapter Five, which looks at the imaginative and strikingly varied reuse of old buildings.

This is a time of ferment in planning, design, and land development, a time when what once seemed enlightened is being subjected to reappraisal. If Frank Lloyd Wright and other influential designers in the first half of the twentieth century succeeded in shifting the focus of houses toward the seclusion of the backyard, some of today's architects are intent on re-emphasizing the house's responsibility for enhancing the life on the streets and sidewalks—for bringing a human and architectural presence to the neglected public domain. If every suburban developer in the 1970s seemed to imagine himself or herself a latter-day (though not so ambitious) Frederick Law Olmsted, curving the streets and rejecting the supposed harshness of the grid plan, dissenting design professionals now ask whether the curved street and the cul-de-sac are the best solutions we can envisage. Designers raise another fundamental question: should houses be in a separate zone from shops and offices? If not, how can they be organized so that the noise and commotion of commerce don't disrupt residential life? Questions like these, basic questions that once appeared settled, are being opened to reconsideration.

What's especially intriguing is the combination of innovation and traditionalism in today's houses. Technology marches on, constantly updating the methods and materials on which homebuilding depends. Alterations in the kinds of households being formed and in how people choose to spend their time at home are making houses depart significantly from what used to be customary. The accumulation of change dictates that houses in the remainder of the twentieth century will be different from those that came before.

And yet a certain amount of tradition continues to be prized. Running through many of today's houses is a heightened appreciation of the familiar. Changes are absorbed and turned into integral parts of houses that end up looking not nearly as surprising as might have been expected. An equilibrium is preserved by blending the novel and the traditional. Front porches and Victorian ornamentation show up on houses intended for life in an electronic age. Interest in the shapes and styles of houses that preceded the Modernist movement has never been stronger than it is today. Even institutional housing developments have been designed with clapboard siding and series of gabled roofs—remarkably resembling rows of cottages—to evoke the beloved image of traditional American houses.

At a convention of the National Association of Home Builders in the mid-1980s, the editor of *Builder*, the industry's leading journal, showed hundreds of assembled homebuilders a sketch of a detached house with a peaked roof, a couple of windows on the façade, and a door positioned front and center. The sketch had been drawn by the editor's four-year-old daughter and was offered in all seriousness as inspiration toward the better design of America's houses. This presentation was not an isolated occurrence. The image of the traditional American house is being invoked throughout the country —by ordinary builders and acclaimed architects alike. American houses grow more diverse, more technologically sophisticated, more attuned to new patterns of behavior, and yet strong threads of continuity remain. Many people are now searching for just the right balance between new ways and long-cherished visions of domestic life. It's an interesting time to look at America's houses.

Chapter One

Settings

Seabridge Villas in Huntington Beach, California, embodies the guiding principle of many of today's suburban developments: cluster the housing together more tightly, but offset the dense feeling by focusing the units on a landscape more lush than that of a single-family lot.

The busy road from San Francisco International Airport clings to level expanses of land only a few feet above sea level as it carries its rushing stream of traffic northward toward the city, about 8 miles away. Highway 101, also called the Bayshore Freeway, opts for the horizontal wherever there's a choice of terrain. On its smooth, gradeless pavement, travelers dash without downshifting through a landscape packed with subdivisions, shopping centers, and industrial strips. Not only the highway but most of the man-made development has concentrated on the low, undemanding ground near the bay as the San Francisco Peninsula's population has steadily multiplied.

Just south of the city, the topography along the Bayshore suddenly turns challenging. The San Bruno Mountains abruptly rise several hundred feet, throwing up a high, grassy obstacle to development. The dense accumulation of buildings and streets that extends for nearly 50 miles, all the way from San Jose to San Francisco, only laps at the mountains' base. The slopes are steep, and they remain largely undeveloped, deflecting the low-lying road toward the northeast. They present a refreshing sight, a heartening vestige of nature along the hectic highway.

But the exclusion of construction from the mountainsides is not absolute. In a few places, a line of houses ascends a slope at an unvarying angle, as if the houses had somehow perched on a tightrope held taut against the land. Each row consists of many little houses pressed close together, side by side, their roofs invisible in their near-flatness. From a distance, it's difficult to tell for sure that the houses are covered in stucco, but no matter—it's their colors that stand out, each house a different variety of pastel.

In the early 1960s, Berkeley songwriter Malvina Reynolds was driving just a few miles to the west of this area when she saw, on the slopes, strings of small stucco houses nearly identical to these; the sight inspired her to compose a song, later made famous by Pete Seeger, about "little boxes on the hillside, little boxes made of ticky-tacky, little boxes on the hillside, little boxes all the same." The song's sarcasm was expressed so lightly, in childlike rhythms, that "Little Boxes" became one of the best-loved pieces of modern folk music. Glancing up from Highway 101 at the flimsy-looking houses in the San Brunos, a traveler could be tempted to sing along. "There's a green one and a pink one and a blue one"—and other colors, too, on the slopes of San Francisco's southern perimeter. Constructed during the boom after the Second World War, the little stucco houses convey scant dignity or seriousness.

And yet, anyone who looks with a receptive eye discovers that the houses actually engender feelings quite different from the song's mockery. To the viewer's surprise, the houses possess an undeniable charm, primarily because of their relationship to the land. Their simple, repetitive forms, when set against the rugged backdrop of the hills, suggest an air of delicacy. The dwellings contrast with the land without subjugating it. The mountains retain their strength, and the houses become all the more agreeable because they make a thin, fragile string across a powerful terrain. It's this pattern that makes the houses appealing. If they were scattered at random throughout the hills, they would mar the grandeur of the topography with a visual hodgepodge. The linear compression of the houses on the mountainsides is the source of their compelling attractiveness.

A common lament among architects, builders, and developers has to do with the scarcity of uncomplicated building sites. "The best sites have already been built on" is a refrain heard in Seattle, in Ann Arbor, Michigan, along the Connecticut shore, and in many places in between. The land available now, so goes the complaint, doesn't easily accommodate houses. Yet whoever erected the houses in the San Brunos nearly forty years ago could have said exactly the same thing; the terrain was exceedingly formidable. But, in the end, the homes that were built achieved a satisfying relationship with their setting. There's little doubt that housing in the years ahead will, in many cases, have to cope with irregular sites or adapt to higher population densities, but this does not necessarily imply a disheartening outcome. A wide range of pleasing and imaginative solutions is possible.

To understand the character of what's being built today, it's useful to trace the historical metamorphosis that has taken place in American homebuilding. Traditionally, most American houses took the form of detached structures on individual lots—with the exceptions in cities like New York and Philadelphia. The great majority of local governments long ago made the rectangular grid the basic pattern of development, and blocks, especially in urban areas, tended to be divided into long, thin lots, with the result that the house's narrow dimension faced the street.

Narrow houses and lots presented disadvantages in the twentieth century. Once the automobile became ubiquitous, the prevailing practice was to supply the house with a private driveway that ran from the street in front, along the entire side of the house, to a garage near the back of the lot. By the 1930s, it was clear that this was a wasteful arrangement. The garage and driveway occupied much of the backyard and dominated a side yard. By that time, out-

houses, chicken coops, and other unattractive structures had all but disappeared from backyards, and it was apparent that if the garage could be repositioned, the backyard could be transformed into a pleasant center for family recreation. Some movement toward a new layout took place in the 1930s, and changes arrived on a large scale after the Second World War. Lots were laid out wider and sometimes shallower so that the garage could be placed next to the house or attached to it. The backyard, freed from intrusions, was ready for patios, pools, decks, and, most of all, trees and grass.

Green as the reorganized residential settings were, they still had a somewhat stiff countenance. The grid had been reproportioned, but it had not yet been replaced. What seemed to be required was a second transformation, one whose roots lay in an unlikely source—the so-called rural cemeteries that began to appear on the edges of American cities in the first half of the nineteenth century.

Until early in that century, cemeteries in urban America were typically small and congested with gravestones. But in the 1820s and 1830s, beginning in Boston, cemeteries in larger cities started to be conceived of as pastoral retreats. An 1831 plan for Mount Auburn Cemetery in Cambridge, Massachusetts, called for carriage drives to wind through undulating wooded hills. So popular did such picturesque, naturalistic cemeteries become—not just with people buying burial plots but also with city dwellers seeking a respite from workaday urban life—that the prominent landscape architect Andrew Jackson Downing often cited them as a sign that cities needed parks laid out according to the same principles. Rather than leveling the land and planting it with formal rows of trees and shrubbery, the makers of romantic landscapes wanted to delight in the irregularity of nature. Paths would follow the meandering lay of the land; if the land was by nature flat, well, then the park builders might have to intervene, making knolls and hollows where none had previously existed.

By far the most notable designer of these romantic parks was Frederick Law Olmsted, the landscape architect who planned New York's Central Park in the 1850s and subsequently designed parks and park systems for cities throughout the United States. In 1869, Olmsted received an assignment that differed from his usual work: he was asked to plan Riverside, Illinois, a residential community in what would later become a burgeoning western suburb of Chicago. There he eliminated curbs, and he set the streets in slight depressions to make the pavement less conspicuous and to focus attention on the landscape. The road system followed a series of gradual curves—the better, said Olmsted, to suggest "leisure, contemplativeness, and happy tranquillity."

Riverside turned out to be overambitious—a financial failure—and most of America's residential areas continued to favor the relentless right angle. But the charm of a landscape whose vistas constantly changed as the viewer moved through a succession of gentle curves was ultimately not to be denied. After a gestation period of more than three-quarters of a century, the meandering street system finally won acceptance in a huge number of suburban developments built after the Second World War. Inevitably, the lots in such subdivisions were often smaller than what Olmsted had envisioned, and many of the subtleties of his approach also eluded the average developer. But on the whole, a more informal atmosphere took root. This manner of planning, as it was eventually modified and elaborated on, introduced a graduated system of roads, from cul-de-sacs, which fostered neighborliness and eliminated unwanted traffic; to loop roads, which also discouraged outsiders from speeding through; to "collector" roads that accommodated movement within the development; to thoroughfares that carried the heavy traffic of the larger region. Detached houses generally faced the less traveled roads, while other kinds of structures—sometimes including apartment buildings occupied predominantly by people without children—lay closer to the heavier traffic. Handled skillfully, this mode of planning could—in comparison to the grid—enhance safety and engender a certain relaxed feeling within a community. This is the kind of arrangement that most Americans expect to find when they look at suburban houses.

It is a pattern, however, that is undergoing a squeeze. In 1949, developed land (ground that has been graded and supplied with utilities and roads) accounted for about 11 percent of the cost of the average new house. By 1969, this figure had nearly doubled, to 21 percent of the house's price, and by 1982 it had risen still further, to 24 percent. Some builders have compensated by making the lots narrower and shallower, but most have refused to budge from their basic concept—individual houses set in curvilinear subdivisions. A chief pitfall of this is that even when suburban lots measured, say, 80 by 130 feet and everyone had a front yard, a backyard, and two side yards, the sense of a truly natural landscape often survived only weakly. When the size of the lots shrank, the landscape's graciousness dwindled even more. With houses of similar design on one lookalike bend after another, it became all too apparent that curvilinear streets could be as monotonous as rectilinear ones. Another method of meshing house and land was needed, and it began to flourish in the 1960s in a number of places, many of them on the West Coast.

Ground-level commercial space at Two Worlds in Mountain View, California, recedes from the view of townhouses above. Commercial areas are close to home, yet inconspicuous.

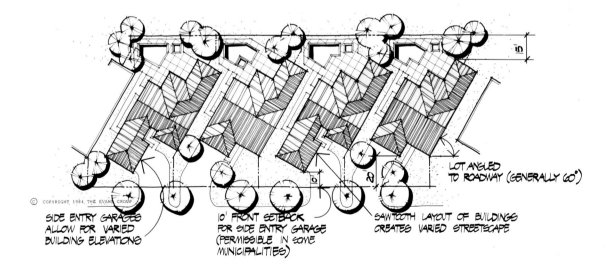

© COPYRIGHT 1984 THE EVANS GROUP

SIDE ENTRY GARAGES ALLOW FOR VARIED BUILDING ELEVATIONS

10' FRONT SETBACK FOR SIDE ENTRY GARAGE (PERMISSIBLE IN SOME MUNICIPALITIES)

SAWTOOTH LAYOUT OF BUILDINGS CREATES VARIED STREETSCAPE

LOT ANGLED TO ROADWAY (GENERALLY 60°)

Staggered zero-lot-line houses, like these by The Evans Group, present a varied appearance on the street, and they permit longer views than otherwise would be expected from the entrance through the house to pleasant outdoor areas at the rear.

In 1964 two young San Francisco architects, A. Robert Fisher and Rodney F. Friedman, formed a partnership and began working with suburban housing developers and municipalities, though they knew that this was hardly the accepted route to renown in the architectural profession. (Among architects who concentrate on residential design, eminence tends to go to those who produce one-of-a-kind houses for an elite clientele; tract housing, though often declared to be in desperate need of greater design talent, is a field that most prominent architects diligently avoid, as if they might be tainted by contact with the tastes of mass-market developers and homebuyers.)

An interesting challenge awaited them: how to design housing for higher, more economical densities and at the same time create a more satisfying environment? Routine planning and zoning ordinances had been fairly rigid, stipulating what type of housing could be placed where—specifying a certain number of detached houses per acre, for instance, and regulating their size and placement on the lots. Fisher-Friedman Associates helped to write guidelines for some of the alternatives then being initiated—planned-unit developments, or PUDs. The PUDs were extensive tracts, usually in suburbs or resort areas, where municipalities gave the developers more flexibility than standard ordinances permitted. Developers obtained permission to build denser-than-usual housing in some sections of their property, and they gained a freer hand in determining where the housing would be placed. In return for such concessions, the developer treated the environment more thoughtfully than would have been the case under ordinary zoning. Usually the developer preserved or enhanced an important natural feature—a pond, a portion of waterfront, a scenic stand of woods. Instead of parceling out all the land as individual houselots, the development kept some of its property as common open space and typically allocated parts of its land to different forms of housing —detached houses in some areas and higher-density housing, such as apartment buildings and townhouses, elsewhere. Developers frequently found this procedure advantageous because it allowed a greater total number of housing units and, by clustering much of the housing in compact areas, saved money on moving earth, paving streets, and installing utilities.

Along with more sensitive treatment of the land, a more sophisticated marketing approach also arrived. Research enabled architects to design a varied range of housing that would appeal to specific segments of the populace, instead of making all the houses conform to the same mold. Fisher-Friedman became one of a new breed of professional firms, getting involved in the planning and construction processes early, helping decide which portions of the land to build on, recommending the kinds of housing appropriate to both the site and the market, and then designing the houses. Fisher-Friedman was not alone. Other architectural firms that carved out this more comprehensive responsibility also rose to prominence. They included Sandy & Babcock in San Francisco, Barry Berkus's Berkus Group Architects in Santa Barbara, California, and Danielian Associates and Richardson Nagy Martin, both in Newport Beach, California.

Similar firms appeared in other parts of the country, but without a doubt the best-known firms—the ones that became design leaders for the homebuilding industry—were concentrated largely in California, a state with an extraordinary growth rate and a receptive attitude toward design innovation. The cost of development in

California was escalating faster than in many other parts of the country, so there was a strong incentive to find acceptable ways of raising the density of housing. And not least important, California claimed unusual landowners like the Irvine Company, which controlled an immense territory of 75,000 acres of agricultural land —about a sixth of Orange County—that lay directly in the path of Los Angeles's south-eastward expansion. The Irvine Company was going to spend more than twenty years turning its citrus groves, cropland, and cattle country into residential communities. This called for a higher level of skill than homebuilders and developers could supply by themselves. Fisher-Friedman, Berkus Group, Danielian Associates, and Richardson Nagy Martin all received commissions from the Irvine Company.

The new relationship of the architect–land planner to homebuilding, now common in California, unfortunately is less prevalent elsewhere in the country. Though there are comparable organizations farther east—like The Evans Group in Orlando, Florida, and Land Design Research in Columbia, Maryland, and land-planning organizations like David Jensen Associates in Denver and Matarazzo Design in Concord, New Hampshire, which lay out subdivisions but generally do not design the houses —much suburban homebuilding in the eastern and central sections of the country muddles along without benefit of sophisticated design professionals. But what has evolved in California is clearly going to become more common throughout the country as costs increase, as environmental consciousness makes an impact, and as the Californians' accomplishments become better known. One sign of this trend is the remarkable volume and geographic scope of the Californians' work. Barry Berkus's organization has undertaken projects in more than

25 states. In a little more than two decades, Fisher-Friedman has planned or designed well over 100,000 housing units across the country. And while much of the profession's recognition continues to go to designers of unique houses that boast striking stylistic twists, Fisher-Friedman has won scores of architectural awards for housing built at six to fifty units to the acre.

Today's PUDs are often smaller than those of the late 1960s and early 1970s, and they're generally less likely to provide clubhouses and other expensive community facilities. But a central principle of the PUD—the clustering of housing on portions of the site where it makes economic, ecological, and architectural sense—has gained acceptance in a growing number of cities and towns. As designers are called on to deal with difficult pieces of land, they increasingly concentrate the dwellings on only part of the property, leaving other areas free of construction. The concept of clustering is used even where the property is not formally designated a PUD.

To see a development like Windswept, on the South Carolina coast, is to appreciate the advantages of this more imaginative approach to the land. In 1981, a developer asked Sandy & Babcock to design oceanfront resort condominiums on Kiawah Island, an unspoiled, low-lying barrier island south of Charleston. In some coastal resorts, including part of the exclusive community of Palm Beach, Florida, developers had lined beaches with undistinguished, blocky white buildings that dominate the landscape and cut off many views of the ocean; the desire to get as much money as possible from every square foot of oceanfront land largely destroyed the natural setting that made the site attractive in the first place. In South Carolina, the Kiawah

Inside a condominium unit at Windswept, zigzagging
walls with well-placed windows open up long views of
Kiawah Island, South Carolina, and the Atlantic Ocean.
At the same time, the staggered walls break the exterior
of the complex into rhythmic segments with individual
sitting areas overlooking the water.

Island Company, as developer, insisted on putting a profitable 90 units on 13½ acres but asked Sandy & Babcock to make the buildings reasonably unobtrusive. High-rises were ruled out. The architects designed three- to five-story clusters of condominiums with copper-finished roofs and red cedar-shingled walls to harmonize with the rustic surroundings. They also gave the buildings irregular silhouettes tapering outward toward ground level. Wall surfaces were broken into smaller segments by a succession of indentations and extensions, reducing the buildings' bulk and giving the complex a more romantic, picturesque character. Because of the staggered silhouette, people behind the buildings get more glimpses of the ocean. Clustering the condominiums on only a portion of the site enables Windswept to preserve the dunes in their original condition. Inside the apartments, the designers arranged "view corridors" so that anyone entering an apartment can immediately see to the end of the living room and then out to the Atlantic or down a 10-mile-long beach. More decks and balconies command vistas of water and beach than would have been possible from a rectangular building. In addition, placement of these terraces in the recesses and projections guarantees residents a certain amount of privacy.

Windswept's dramatic location may be out of the ordinary, but its architectural and planning concepts are not. The staggered profile has become almost a standard element in the design of attached housing, partly because it makes the building a less rigid presence in the landscape, partly because it gives the building a more human scale. Rarely does a condominium cluster have long straight walls that drop without interruption from peak to earth. More often, extensions poke out from the core of the building as it approaches the ground. People often

feel more at ease with a large building if its periphery terminates in segments that are relatively narrow and only a story or two high—comfortable dimensions to stand next to. In addition to making a big building more friendly, the irregular "footprint" gives each household a sense of possessing its own definable, individualized part of the complex—a home whose bounds are clearly demarcated.

The strategy of breaking the building into distinct, identifiable household units is not restricted to properties that are owned by their occupants, although that's where it most strongly predominates. Some government-subsidized rental complexes have also adopted the staggered profile and the irregular footprint, reflecting the belief that residents will be happier with housing that affirms their individuality. A complex that steps in and out also presents practical advantages for outdoor living. The zigzag has become a dominant shape of our time.

If irregular silhouettes make clustered housing feel softer and smaller, this does not imply that these complexes necessarily disappear into the landscape. Though meant to be unintimidating at close range, these complexes are also designed to make a strong, memorable, marketable impression from a distance. One of the most noticeable things about clusters of suburban or rural housing is that, at their best, they establish a distinctive rhythm on the horizon, confidently proclaiming their presence, sometimes in harmony with the texture of the land, sometimes in contrast to it.

The intention of making a visual statement becomes clear with a glance at the rooftops of these complexes. These are active, intricate compositions that punctuate the sky. No TV antennas are permitted here—the architects know well that rooftops can trumpet the personality of a residential complex just as a jazzy metallic spire announces the character of New York's Chrysler Building. Indeed, the lasting impression of many suburban complexes is of chimneys on the horizon; they've become as important to a condominium complex as a steeple is to a New England village church. Looking at the more visually dazzling condominiums around the country, you can almost imagine the architects reserving their most intense deliberation for the question of how to design a more visually effective chimney and, more important, a better chimney cap—a cap that will play well against the forms of the buildings below, a cap that will move the eye in the direction the architect wants it to go, a cap that will strike just the right note on the horizon. Ours is an era of chimney-cap architecture. Build a better chimney cap, and condo buyers might just beat a path to the sales office.

Clustered housing, by casting a picturesque outline against the sky, is capable of achieving a scale in balance with a natural setting, especially when there are hills, ravines, rivers, or other features against which the housing can become a visual counterpoint. Where a series of freestanding houses may merely subdue the land, dividing it into insignificant parcels, a concentration of attached houses can generate a stimulating tension between what's been created by nature and what's been made by the effort of man.

Quite a different kind of question is raised by the land immediately surrounding a house. How should it be handled? Strongly conflicting approaches are being implemented today, and they reflect decades of disagreement about the best way to develop the residential landscape. At the turn of the century, the intellectual historian Vernon L. Parrington found it mystifying that many Americans would choose to live in houses whose grounds seemed almost deliberately designed to inhibit privacy. At that time, the typical house had a main porch that was positioned along the front, exposed to strangers' glances—a location Parrington considered illogical. He proposed that the outdoor living area of the house focus toward the rear, where there would be an attractive yard with hedges, shrubs, or other features to shield it from neighbors' eyes. By contrast, Frank J. Scott, an influential writer on suburban gardening, argued that the land around suburban houses—both front and back—should be a visually uninterrupted expanse, enhancing everyone's enjoyment by providing pleasingly long vistas. Unless barriers remained minimal, Scott said, people would "deprive themselves of what costs them nothing and profits them much."

Today what usually shows up in neighborhoods of detached houses, especially in the Northeast and Midwest, is a combination of Parrington's and Scott's points of view. Outdoor life focuses almost entirely on the backyard, but often it's a yard open to everyone's gaze. Granted, there really is something congenial about an expansive view of grassy lawns—even when it includes a few swing sets, barbecue grills, and other backyard paraphernalia—but the openness needs some balance. There should be some small outdoor areas to offer relief from constant exposure. What's especially surprising is that much of the attached housing now being built in the Northeast and Midwest is set in landscapes just as open as those associated with detached houses, even though attached housing doesn't provide distance from neighbors to serve as a buffer. A rethinking is needed. One compromise solution, used especially in townhouse developments in New England, is to install lattice or other attractively detailed fences

33

Houses today may hug an urban waterfront, enjoy terraces around a rooftop courtyard, cultivate an "edible landscape," or use a flat terrain as the base for a dramatic architectural ascent. Arizona houses sometimes merge with the vastness

that extend from the back of the complex for 10 to 20 feet, giving each household a semiprivate outdoor area. Beyond these individual patios and gardens, a grassy landscape continues uninterrupted, tying the setting together. In time, dense shrubbery can accomplish much the same objective, forming enclaves amid a cohesive environment.

In California and some other parts of the Sunbelt, builders often provide private outdoor areas for detached houses by constructing 6-foot-high walls around the entire backyard. (A favorite material for these walls is "slump-stone"—a concrete block that bears some resemblance to adobe.) Walled outdoor areas are

a centuries-old tradition in hot climates, and they do make for enjoyable living. The problem is that they obliterate the sense of being part of an overall environment.

The wholly walled-off houselot isn't something that deserves to be exported to the rest of the country. What the residents of the Northeast, Midwest, and other regions might profit from more is the patio home—a design that builders began popularizing in the 1960s and 1970s to provide agreeable surroundings on smaller lots. Many patio homes are crescent- or U-shaped so as to focus on a semienclosed outdoor area. On a small lot, this may be almost all the usable outdoor space a household gets.

of the desert, while southern California houses, like the zero-lot-line houses (this page, top left), *concentrate on making the most of narrow side lots.*

But this is such a serviceable configuration that it need not be relegated solely to small lots. On properties of ordinary size, it supplies a protected outdoor place equally well. And a conventional floor plan need not be rearranged much to provide this kind of layout. Just pushing an attached garage back so that it extends from a rear corner of the house can easily provide one side wall for the semiprivate area.

Where lot sizes have to be reduced, patio homes offer one alternative that does not involve too much loss of livability. Some patio homes have been designed with one wall left windowless and positioned against a side property line, allowing the next-door neighbor to have a side

yard with a high degree of privacy. Entire blocks of detached houses on small lots can be laid out this way, each house pushed to one of its side boundaries so that every residence commands a secluded side court. This idea, known as "zero-lot-line" planning, has won broad acceptance in California, Florida, and other parts of the Sunbelt in the 1980s. The distance between houses may be as little as 10 feet, and if the strip is divided between two neighbors — each owning 5 feet of it — it serves little use except as a buffer zone. Zero-lot-line planning, by placing each side lot under one household's control, seizes the potential of land that would otherwise have gone mostly to waste.

35

The shapes of zero-lot-line houses vary considerably from one subdivision to another. Some houses sit with their narrow end to the street, the outdoor space extending along one side and across the back in an L shape. The entrance is typically placed on the side, where a landscaped courtyard provides a gracious sense of arrival. If the entrance path is made to meander a little, the side court can be hidden behind a wall or plantings. In the Vista Filare subdivision in Irvine, California, detached zero-lot-line houses with side-court entrances were placed on lots averaging 36 feet wide and 86 feet deep. Such lots do not feel generous, but they are enjoyable, primarily because they offer seclusion.

Many zero-lot-line houses on rectangular properties give the street a conspicuous row of garage doors or require a rear alley lined with garages. To avoid the monotony of either of these solutions and to further enhance the house and its outdoor areas, architects and planners have devised a number of variations on the zero-lot-line concept. At the Scottsdale Ranch outside Phoenix, Richardson Nagy Martin designed "staggered zero-lot-line" houses with sawtooth plotting. Each house was placed at an oblique angle to the street, eliminating long straight views of parallel house fronts and rows of garage doors. With the irregularly angled lots, visitors still enter some houses by way of attractive side courts. The kitchen or living room or family room and the master bedroom open onto outdoor areas toward the rear of the house. The angled configuration also creates views that extend diagonally through the house —from the entrance through the living room and out into the rear court, where careful planting can create an appealing focal point and alleviate the feeling of being boxed in. In addition, a staggered configuration can eliminate the need to leave one entire wall devoid of windows.

With zero-lot-line planning, detached houses can be built at eight or nine units to the acre. Some developers construct them at even higher densities, but many designers believe that the lots then feel cramped and that another form of housing should be constructed instead. Often the alternative is a townhouse (generally known as a row house before it was semantically upgraded). If the budget is generous and the climate is mild, the townhouse can have its interior organized around an atrium. The amount of land enclosed by the atrium need not be large; even a small area, when placed at the core of the house, can be a spectacular focal point. If the house's entrance is positioned adjacent to the atrium, it generates a dramatic sense of arrival: you open the door and find plants and sunlight in a little oasis directly in front of you. The central atrium can visually connect all the rooms on one level, thus enhancing the feeling of spaciousness, yet at the same time it can separate the rooms and prevent sounds from traveling as easily as they would in a thoroughly open interior. Some atriums have four glass-enclosed sides arranged to face the entrance, kitchen, dining area, and living room respectively. On the upper level of a two-story townhouse, the atrium can help to illuminate bedrooms and bathrooms.

In larger buildings, atriums can be expanded to gigantic size. In Tampa, Florida, the local firm of Rowe Holmes Barnett Architects designed a twenty-two-story luxury condominium tower whose lobby is set in a naturally ventilated atrium that rises to the top of the building. When residents go from the elevators to their apartments, they walk through open corridors at the perimeter of the atrium. Windows and doors of the apartments can open into the atrium or into nearby corridors, obtaining a cross-ventilation that's unusual in high-rise buildings.

Some of the units even have balconies overlooking the atrium.

For complexes composed of townhouses or apartments stacked several stories high, enclosure of part of the landscape is a dramatic feature. In Palo Alto Redwoods, a condominium complex that Fisher-Friedman designed in Palo Alto, California, and in Seabridge Villas, a rental complex designed by Danielian Associates in Huntington Beach, California, three to four floors of living units are stacked above the parking garage. In both complexes, the buildings wrap around a landscaped core.

Noisy streets and unappealing views are some of the most common reasons for shifting attention toward a central area that can be generously planted and made a major attraction. One side of Seabridge Villas is exposed to noise from a busy highway. At Palo Alto Redwoods, one edge borders the rear parking lot of a twenty-four-hour restaurant on heavily traveled El Camino Real. At difficult sites being developed as townhouses, "stacked flats," and other moderately dense kinds of housing, environmental problems like these are not uncommon. The central landscaped area becomes an important advantage, offering residents a refreshing contrast to the world outside.

The semienclosed landscape is an idea with a long pedigree. Many of the finest urban apartment buildings at the start of the twentieth century adopted a U shape, with an elaborate formal entrance placed at the end of a long, well-landscaped walk flanked by the building's symmetrical wings. This arrangement supplied the apartments with light and air at the same time that it dignified the act of entering and leaving the building. Some apartments and condominiums continue to be laid out as symmetrical or near-symmetrical complexes around rectangular courtyards (though rarely with the grandeur of the classically inspired buildings of

eighty years ago). Today tastes run more toward informality, and the courtyards often avoid following straight lines. The prevailing mode is a meander. Sometimes a natural feature or an irregularly shaped site provides a rationale for the meander. In Palo Alto Redwoods, the walkways in the center court twist around tall redwoods that the designers were careful to preserve. But even when such strong natural features are absent, meandering layouts are often chosen anyway, because they offer a changing series of views to people walking through the complex; especially in a large development, the bends and turns in the walkways help to offset an institutional feeling.

The U-shaped buildings of several decades ago placed the walkway precisely in the center, and by doing so, they kept foot traffic away from the windows that looked onto the courtyard. To get from the building entrance to an apartment's door, of course, visitors and residents had to walk down interior hallways. The emphasis today, especially in complexes owned by their occupants, is on replacing common corridors with individual household entrances that open directly onto the courtyard. This provides more privacy for units on the ground floor, but, ironically, it can reduce the privacy for those above. It's easy enough to place common walkways some distance from windows on the ground floor, but how can this be accomplished on upper levels? Some complexes are built with bridge systems that connect each upper-level apartment to a main walkway at least 10 feet from windows and doors. The problem is that bridge systems are expensive. To reduce costs, upper-level walkways more often run right next to the windows and doors (much as in an economy motel!). And although designers attempt to position living rooms and bedrooms away from the walkways, there are limits to how successful this strategy can be; in

Gateways and ceremonial entrances are proliferating today, enhancing the sense of arrival both at large complexes like *Palo Alto Redwoods* (above) *and at individual houses like the one designed by William H. Grover* (left). *At Palo Alto Redwoods, the vehicular gate begins an entry procession that culminates with people walking on meandering paths amid preserved redwood trees.*
OPPOSITE
The excitement of entering a condominium tower in Tampa, Florida, springs from its 22-story atrium.

an open-plan interior, even a kitchen window can allow passers-by to see into part of the living room. The prospective occupant has to consider whether the advantages—such as the homelike feeling of direct access to the outdoors —outweigh the drawbacks. Courtyard complexes with individual entrances certainly offer more light and cross-ventilation than do most buildings with internal corridors, and, as a visit to a courtyard complex will attest, many residents cope with the privacy question simply by shutting the blinds when they're concerned about who might glance in.

There's no doubt that many more complexes will be designed around a central landscape, especially in regions with warm climates. Some such courtyards that have already been built are furnished with a refreshing array of pools, fountains, plantings, and other amenities, all hidden from the eyes of outsiders. Access to the courtyard can be controlled through a few gates, so the landscape is not only attractive; it's also secure—an important point for the single people and couples who are the predominant occupants of these complexes.

The protected courtyard arrangement lends itself not only to higher-density suburban development but to housing in downtown areas as well. It is one answer to the question of how to create housing on deep urban blocks—blocks that, if developed to a uniform height from one street to another, could not offer cross-ventilation and natural light to the units in their core. An imaginative application of the courtyard technique is Seattle's South Arcade, a downtown block containing three contiguous new buildings designed by the local firm of Olson/Walker Architects.

From the exterior, the South Arcade looks like a traditional urban block, each building set against the walls of its neighbors and lined up tight against the public sidewalks. On the interior, though, striking departures from the ordinary become apparent. Running through the ground floor of all three buildings is a commercial arcade that leads into the famous Pike Place Market, a sprawling old structure bustling with fish and produce stands, food vendors, flower shops, and gift stores. Above the arcade is housing—in different shapes and sizes for a varied clientele. One building, containing luxury condominiums, is laid out with a round opening at its core. Next to it is an apartment building reserved for the elderly; its core is a large rectangular courtyard one level up from the arcade. The doors of the three stories of apartments in this building face onto open-air corridors that encircle the courtyard. The centerpiece of the courtyard is a garden with multiple levels, where residents can relax outdoors in security. Nearby between Pike Place Market and a noisy waterfront highway, Olson/Walker designed a condominium complex, Hillclimb Court, whose apartments and decks face a communal courtyard offering a similar combination of quiet and safety.

A few blocks away stands a new building, Waterfront Place, that features townhouselike units grouped around a courtyard. What sets Waterfront Place apart is that the townhouses, three stories of them, sit on top of ten floors of stores, restaurants, offices, and parking facilities. Bumgardner Architects of Seattle organized this building so that at ground level, residents enter a conservatively appointed lobby with locked doors; riding an elevator to another formal lobby on the eleventh floor, they then walk into their courtyard in the sky. Around the courtyard are a cluster of one- and two-story residential units that afford a choice of prospects —private balconies looking out across downtown Seattle or Puget Sound and patios and decks that look onto the interior courtyard.

San Francisco boasts yet another variation on the concept of a courtyard-in-the-air. On land next to the city's financial district, Fisher-Friedman designed Golden Gateway Commons — three full blocks of red-brick-veneered buildings with stores and offices on their lower two levels and apartments and townhouses above. At one edge of the complex, the elevated Embarcadero Expressway rises almost as high as the apartments and comes within 9 feet of them. The surroundings are noisy — enough so that a glass-block sound wall has been constructed at one corner of Golden Gateway and windows have been fitted with gasketed, double-glazed, acoustic-rated glass. But the courtyards offer a quiet escape from all the commotion. Elevated outdoor walkways from the adjoining Embarcadero Center office complex and elevators from street level bring residents into handsome, well-maintained courtyards with meandering paths bordered by flowers and other vegetation that lead to the apartments. The condominiums' patios are secluded behind walls along the edges of the courtyards; they ensure a full measure of privacy.

One of the striking features of condominium complexes placed above office buildings is their strong similarity to the more earthbound attached housing of the suburbs. The walls facing the courtyards in Golden Gateway Commons and Waterfront Place jog in and out, remarkably like the walls of hundreds of suburban complexes — or like the walls of Windswept, off the South Carolina coast. Paths are anything but straight; a walk that winds among flowers and greenery is more romantic. The goal is to avoid an atmosphere of severity. Fisher-Friedman and many others contend that when residents walk out of their homes, even downtown condos, they shouldn't find themselves in a Manhattan-like environment where hard surfaces rise without a break from sidewalk to sky. Walls should be fragmented into smaller segments, successively set back and relieved with generous planting. A soft green landscape has a texture more amiable than most buildings — even if architects, with their love of structure, traditionally have had trouble accepting this fact. At Golden Gateway Commons, vines were planted soon after construction was complete. "The idea is to get the ivy growing up the whole building someday," Rodney Friedman observed. "I want you to stand next to landscaping instead of vertical walls. When they're covered with vegetation, walls become very benign."

Golden Gateway feels as if it might be a suburban complex that a squadron of helicopters somehow picked up and dropped intact on downtown roofs. It is *in* the city, but not *of* the city. It enjoys access to the attractions of the central business district, but it allows its inhabitants to dodge many of the city's irritations and dangers. Well-crafted blue steel gates at the edges of the pedestrian bridges, along with security codes programmed into the locks of the elevator lobbies, ensure that the rest of the city will enter the meandering courtyards only when authorized. Safety and soothing scenery — these are important attributes of suburban housing, and they're coming to be associated with certain urban residential developments as well.

What several new projects are trying to achieve is a new balance between urban and suburban, between strictly residential functions and other important aspects of life. There's growing interest in bringing together employment, retailing, and housing, but in ways that still keep these elements distinct from one

TOP
Seattle's South Arcade, where shared courtyards are sheltered from the street.

BELOW
The tranquil patio is a natural extension of a condo unit in Seattle's high-rise Waterfront Place.

OPPOSITE
A framework of concrete, softened by plants, focuses the view out across Puget Sound from Olson/Walker's Pike and Virginia Building.

another. Many of the leading examples of this trend are on the West Coast. In Mountain View, California, a suburb more than 30 miles south of San Francisco, Bay Area architect Donald MacDonald arranged 62 townhouses and 20,000 square feet of commercial space on 4 acres along El Camino Real, demonstrating another way to combine, yet separate, housing and commercial activity. The stores in this complex, constructed of concrete and concrete-filled block, face the heavily traveled street; their roofs are made of concrete 10 inches thick— strong enough to support plazas above. It's on these plazas that most of the townhouses sit, sequestered from the activity below. Because of the overhangs of the concrete roofs, the residents don't see the commercial areas from their homes or even from the plazas. The relationship between housing and business, not only in Mountain View but in other cities and suburbs, is summed up in this development's name: Two Worlds.

The idea of putting new urban housing in the same complex with offices, retailing, and entertainment owes much to Chicago architect Bertrand Goldberg, who in 1959 proposed Marina City, a pioneering "mixed-use" development in downtown Chicago. In the late 1950s, the reigning idea among urban planners was that cities had to be divided into zones—manufacturing in one zone, offices and stores in another, housing in yet another. These neat divisions were supposed to make a more orderly, manageable city; their effect, however, was to aggravate the inner city's loss of population. Goldberg recognized—earlier than many others in the design field—that the city would be more vital if people lived in the central business district. And so, with the backing of the Chicago Flat Janitors Union, which saw its future linked to urban living and consequently invested its pension

money in the project, Goldberg constructed a pair of 65-story cylinders that stand like concrete corncobs along the Chicago River, north of the Loop. Marina City, completed in the early 1960s, provided parking on 18 stories of spiraling ramps. Above the cars rose 896 middle-income apartments. In a lobby at the towers' base and in other buildings on the 3-acre site, Goldberg designed offices, restaurants, shops, bowling alleys, movie theaters, and other diversions. Marina City offered much-needed evidence that Americans financially capable of moving to the suburbs would settle in the city center if their apartments had access to a wide range of amenities.

Marina City seems small in comparison to some of the projects built or proposed in the 1980s. Several blocks to the southwest of Marina City, and within walking distance of Chicago's financial district, a new complex of 4 bulky 49-story buildings, Presidential Towers, boasts 2,346 apartments. This development, covering two square blocks, also contains 100,000 square feet of commercial space, an elaborate health club, and parking for 1,000 cars.

In New York in 1985, developer Donald Trump announced his intention to build nearly 8,000 housing units along with 3.6 million square feet of television and movie studios, technical centers, and offices on former Penn Central Railroad yards along the Hudson River. The project, he said, would boast a 13-block waterfront promenade on the Upper West Side of Manhattan and would have a 3-level, 1.7-million-square-foot shopping center with a public park on its roof. The nearly 8,000 condominium and rental apartments in "Television City," as Trump dubbed his development, would be housed in 6 buildings, each 76 stories high, and in one gigantic 2,600-unit skyscraper soaring 150 stories. Critics quickly saw the proposal as a bargaining ploy aimed at softening people up for a project less mammoth but still beyond any normal, human scale. Even in upward-thrusting Manhattan, no one has yet built such tall residential structures, and a 1,670-foot, 150-story residential tower would doubtless be uneconomical, even if it were to receive the required city approval. Whatever is ultimately built will be considerably lower than Trump's grandiose original projection. The significant fact, however, is that the concept of combining housing with offices, retail stores, and other facilities has gained acceptance. The idea is no longer just the province of visionary architects like Bertrand Goldberg. Many developers, including some of the most influential in New York, now think in terms of mixed-use complexes.

Goldberg himself, meanwhile, has continued to challenge accepted notions about the proper setting for urban life. In 1984, his second big mixed-use project broke ground—this one in Chicago, south of the Loop. On former rail-yards along the Chicago River—and partly over the river itself—a serpentine complex of concrete, River City, began to stretch out. It's a development with many elements: underground parking; a marina; three floors that contain offices, shopping, an auditorium and conference center, educational facilities, a health club, and other services; and, at the top, 8 to 15 stories of apartments that are arranged along a winding, 30-foot-wide interior walkway. Goldberg set out to create "a city within a city," and this is indeed an urban development with a distinctive architectural form. The residential section—initially 446 rental apartments, with plans for an eventual total of 2,500 units—is tied together by the curving interior walkway, an atriumlike structure that reaches up to a roof of

poured concrete interspersed with glass blocks through which sunlight streams in.

From across the river, it's a strange and formidable-looking assemblage. Apartments bulge outward in a succession of bowed concrete walls, their windows set in curved voids oddly suggestive of organ pipes. It's an eerie kind of architectural music that Goldberg has composed; the rhythms of his concrete work are unconventional and not very comforting. The building meanders, but it's so immense and so peculiar-looking that the rambling silhouette only seems to emphasize its bulk further. The structure dominates any puny human beings standing underneath its strutting concrete framework. There's no illusion at River City about providing private, individualized dwellings.

Yet Goldberg's conception should not be dismissed out of hand. The glass-block roof rising as much as 84 feet above the interior walkway is spectacular, and Goldberg's commitment to bringing together living quarters, employment, education, and services deserves high praise. One objective measure of River City is its demonstrated success in appealing to a range of tenants; the complex has attracted people paying rents that range from a little over $600 a month for a studio to $1,600 for a three-bedroom townhouse to $3,600 for the most sought-after penthouses. Above all else, Goldberg merits admiration because in a real estate industry that often proceeds with extreme architectural caution, he has come forth with a genuinely imaginative idea and persisted long enough to see it built. Instead of sticking with concepts that possess an already well-documented marketability, Goldberg has given the housing field an important opportunity to explore alternatives. River City could become a source of ideas that will be incorporated into others' projects in the

The convex concrete forms of Bertrand Goldberg's River City apartment towers undulate along the Chicago River (above). In River City's pedestrian concourse (left), sunlight is filtered through a roof of glass blocks in a concrete framework.

OPPOSITE
Marina City, the 3-acre combination of living, working, and entertainment facilities that in the early 1960s began to win acceptance for the idea of mixed-use urban developments.

46

future. Experimentation on this scale is rare and valuable.

One of the least commendable traits of River City is its aloofness from the old neighborhood nearby. The interior walkway—reserved for River City residents—ignores Chicago's long-established grid of public streets and presumably will siphon off the pedestrian traffic that, at its best, makes the city interesting and safe. Goldberg's development harks back to the idealistic arrogance of the Modernist movement of the 1920s, when architects such as Le Corbusier renounced traditional design and tried to reconstruct cities almost from scratch. Le Corbusier envisioned cities made up of widely spaced towers with ample open land at their base. By the 1950s and 1960s, many developers did in fact erect tall buildings separated by plazas or surrounded by green space. But the plazas often remained empty of human activity, and the green space turned into no-man's-land. When big buildings withdrew from the streets and sidewalks, the city lost its vitality. This uncomfortable truth has been obvious for more than a quarter of a century; and therein lies the most serious failing of River City: it sets itself off from the existing city, creating a private circulation system rather than merging into and reinforcing the traditional street pattern. Only when developments channel more of America's everyday life onto the streets and sidewalks can we reasonably expect the public environment to become safe, pleasant, and stimulating.

Fortunately, since the 1960s, designers, planners, and the public as a whole have gained a renewed appreciation of urban buildings that embrace the sidewalk and infuse life into the public domain. Though new buildings often do not fully re-create the traditional city building pattern—in which shopkeepers and residents easily keep an eye on one another's quarters and thus reduce the opportunities for crime—they at least put stores along the street. In New York, tall buildings often contain retail shops at ground level, then a number of floors of offices, and finally several stories devoted to residential use at the top, where the views are longer and the street noise fainter. The buildings can provide living quarters removed from disturbance while at the same time they reinforce the city's physical coherence.

Row houses, after a long period of being out of fashion, are being erected again in cities like Washington and Chicago, and they're also being constructed to a lesser extent in cities like Houston, where they never previously took hold. Even buildings that are not in fact row houses are sometimes reproducing their rhythms along the street. In San Francisco, after a distressing proliferation of bigger and bulkier buildings in the 1960s, the tendency now—encouraged by architect-planners like Daniel Solomon and by changes in the city's zoning code—is to design new buildings that step up and down the hills in small, regular increments with a succession of projecting bays, much like the Victorian homes for which San Francisco is famous. Where row houses are uneconomical to construct, tall buildings can still emulate row-house rhythms and use tops that add interest to the horizon. Both at street level and on the skyline, there's a growing understanding of a building's urban responsibilities.

Throughout the country—and not solely in cities—designers are paying more attention to the effects of new buildings on older buildings

OPPOSITE
New townhouses on Ames Avenue in historic Chautauqua Institution.

48

nearby. Along the shores of Chautauqua Lake in western New York, the Chautauqua Institution, an extraordinarily picturesque resort dating from the last quarter of the nineteenth century, has been coping for several years with the question of how to fit new buildings in among the old wooden houses and hotels. Lawson, Knapp & Pulver—a Rochester, New York, architectural firm—designed a set of new townhouses capturing the characteristic Chautauqua feeling of wooden houses looking out sociably onto shaded streets. Gabled roofs, double-hung windows, and horizontal siding resembling the clapboards of neighboring buildings all help to make the new Ames Avenue townhouses at ease with their setting. In this dense little compound, where cars are banned during the summer and the narrow streets are filled with people strolling, the old buildings abound with porches —as many as four stories of them, giving the community a gregarious atmosphere. The architects consequently put porches on the new townhouses and softened their lines with white-painted railings and decorative brackets. The residents completed the effect by adding old-fashioned striped awnings.

In suburban areas, public responsibilities are much less well understood. A major failing of single-family residential development, especially in California, Arizona, and Florida, is that the community always seems to be receding from view. Subdivisions are built with their backs to the major streets—backs shielded by fences or walls and perhaps softened with some planting. The network of roads that link inhabitants to one another feels drained of any impor-

tance beyond mere functionalism; the roads suggest the fragmentation of the community into a multitude of private domains. A visitor searches in vain for a strong focal point, for something that seems to offer a public welcome. Even after leaving the main roads and heading onto the side streets, one senses that the public domain still projects a kind of emptiness, the houses turning their attention toward hidden backyards, walled side yards, enclosed courtyards. Thousands of streets have a polite yet forlorn atmosphere—quiet and undemanding, but unable to give people a sense of occupying a stage where their presence matters. The ultimate acknowledgment of this is the decision not even to install sidewalks, there being no reason to stroll in such barren surroundings. What does serve as a visual "event" is the subdivision entrance, especially if it's embellished with generous landscaping or gates. In Sunbelt subdivisions in particular, the entrance calls for an impressive set of gates (with or without an accompanying gatehouse). The gates are meant more as an expression of privacy and status than as a celebration of a public realm, however.

Scattered imaginative attempts have been made to invest tract developments with inviting public areas. In the West Fairacres Village subdivision in Omaha, Nebraska, Daniel Solomon and John Goldman designed houses in a bungalow style reminiscent of the 1920s, each house with an ample porch facing the street. The porches, each using a different assembly of parts to achieve a varied appearance, are civic gestures; they help to give the public domain a welcoming atmosphere, making it clear that the public environment has not been forgotten. The private backyard has not been neglected either; the interior is oriented to focus mostly toward it. Fairacres Village strikes a happy balance between private and public, positioning porches **51** and doors so that they address the street, making the shared environment feel more cared for.

Similarly, in Washington, D.C., the local architect Arthur Cotton Moore gave a dignified character to streets in a detached-house subdivision that was built on a 25-acre estate once owned by Nelson Rockefeller. Moore laid out a network of curving streets that enabled the subdivision's 100 houses to avoid ruining the rolling topography. That in itself isn't unusual; what set the development apart was a decision to give the initial group of houses convex or concave façades that echo and reinforce the curves of the streets. From the ends of the façades, fences extend parallel with the street, further helping to define the street. So striking is this conformity of the house shapes to the arcs of the streets that the development was dubbed Foxhall Crescents in reference to the famed Royal Crescent at Bath, England.

One of the most beautiful expressions of order and public-spiritedness in the arranging of the house and its setting is in Boca del Mar, Florida, a quintessentially suburban area where attached housing usually steps in and out, some distance back from curvilinear streets. The staggered, stepped-back profiles can help a complex retire into the background when the natural landscape deserves to be the center of attention, as at Windswept. But when the site is flat and relatively devoid of character, this sort of retreat can degenerate into an exercise in negativism, leaving little in the public environment to be appreciated. The buildings' restlessly irregular positioning undercuts their dignity and sacrifices their ability to define strongly the open space they face. Like a defective container, a meandering complex lets space run out until all that remains between the buildings is a void.

Andres Duany and Elizabeth Plater-Zyberk, architect-planners in Coconut Grove, Florida, decided to design a complex that would avoid such nervous jigging and jogging and the banality that it typically confers on public areas. They studied the old houses of Charleston, South Carolina, especially their relationship to street and land, and applied Charleston's principles to a new subdivision of 111 townhouses on 16 acres in Boca del Mar. Like the old Charleston houses, the new homes in the Florida development—named Charleston Place— are long and narrow, in this case occupying lots that measure 30 feet wide and 88 feet deep from the street in front to a pedestrian path at the rear. The Boca del Mar houses don't have the exposed side porches of the Charleston originals, but they do have side courtyards, and many also have side terraces on the second floor, so they are intricate enough to look interesting even when they're lined up in a row along a straight street. The succession of thin gable ends and narrow recesses on houses that maintain a short, uniform setback from the street serves to shape the public area and enrich it with a satisfying rhythm. The pedestrian paths behind the houses are paved in brick, with walls on each side to guarantee the homeowners' privacy. Roses entwine themselves on trellises above the walks, lending an air of romance.

The houses' shapes are simple and consistent; what distinguishes one house most noticeably from another is color. The architects had intended for all the houses to be white or cream-colored, with dark shutters and trim. Instead the builder called in a color specialist, who saw to it that the houses were painted pink, yellow, orange, and other pastels. Duany thinks the colors detract from the houses' dignity. Actually, though, the varied but light and harmonious colors are the crowning touch, adding a succession

The alternation of one- and two-story elements at Charleston Place in Boca del Mar, Florida, allows for elevated terraces and for ground-level outdoor areas secluded behind walls.

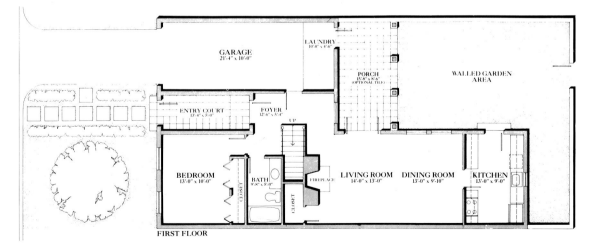

Plan indicates the direct access from kitchen and living room to the garden and porch.

53

By twisting in a succession of sharp angles, the 11,000-square-foot River Oaks house creates a series of views onto an elaborate collection of pools, patios, and other landscape features.

of contrasts that diversify the appearance of Charleston Place without undermining its fundamental orderliness. It's this well-modulated orderliness that gives the complex its essential charm.

This rhythmic, strongly bounded space — characteristic of hundreds, perhaps thousands, of older communities where houses and trees form consistent walls enclosing a straight street — is what's missing from the usual suburban development today. To construct the project as they intended, Duany and Plater-Zyberk had to manipulate many of the standard planning and zoning regulations. Typically a municipality stipulates a minimum width for the street — perhaps 26 or 28 feet — and requires that another

25 feet or so, from the street to the houses' front walls, be left open on either side of it. By the time all the required open ground and paving have been provided, it's often difficult to achieve a sense of enclosure, which depends on establishing the right proportions between the width of the open area and the height of the walls (or, in some instances, trees) that form its visual boundaries. To understand the sense of enclosure, consider the space involved as an outdoor "room." To attain a pleasant sense of enclosure, the room's "floor" must be less than four times as broad as the "walls" — or façades — are high. The most satisfactory ratio, according to landscape architect and author Barrie B. Greenbie, is obtained when the horizontal open

area measures no more than two or three times the walls' height.

To make Charleston Place's design comply with existing regulations, Duany and Plater-Zyberk had to designate the streets as "parking lots," which, according to municipal rules, were not required to stand so far apart from the buildings. The basic urban layout—streets with houses in rows—has become alien to those who are familiar with only cul-de-sacs, loop roads, and curving suburban thoroughfares. As Duany observed of southern Florida, "There's a generation that's grown up here that has never seen a street."

Slowly, progress is being made toward loosening the governmental regulations that have made it difficult for architects and planners, except in a PUD, to produce urbane, fulfilling settings. These rules, though they no doubt deterred some undesirable practices, also jacked up the cost of development. Village Homes, a 260-house subdivision in Davis, California, is one of the developments that demonstrated the potential for breaking free of regulations that did more harm than good. Early in the 1970s, a group of progressives won control of Davis's government, and the municipality allowed Michael N. Corbett to develop Village Homes with a number of departures from standard practice. Ordinarily, a developer has to dig up the property, put down pipe, cover the pipe, and replant on top of it—all so that rain will be carried away underground. Corbett realized that graveled or planted depressions would carry off rainwater on the surface without major problems, and he knew, moreover, that water nearly always makes a landscape more appealing.

The money that Village Homes saved on stormwater systems—about $800 per lot—paid for planting a dozen acres of "edible landscape" —vineyards and plum, peach, cherry, and apricot trees—along pathways and peripheral roads and in an open space near the development's center. The edible landscape in turn provided some food for residents, jobs for teenagers during the harvest season, and money to help organize athletics and other community activities. A single decision—to deal with drainage more or less naturally—ultimately affected the subdivision's appearance, the degree of reliance on commercial food producers, the usefulness of some of the area's youths, social cohesion within Village Homes, and the sense of the manmade environment's connection to the land.

There's no pretending that the thoughtfulness demonstrated at Village Homes predominates throughout the country. Opposing this brand of environmentally conscious planning is a deeply ingrained tradition of engineering-intensive development. The contrast between the two approaches is starkly illustrated in places of great natural beauty like the hill country of Austin, Texas. In parts of northwest Austin, suburban construction has boomed in the 1980s, and conventional development practices have reigned. Whole slopes have lost their natural character under a blanket of houses and streets. As one drives up a steep road, what's conspicuous ahead is not so much the rugged terrain as the fact that it's been put under broad swaths of pavement, which radiate Texas's fierce summertime heat.

On a now-crowded slope in northwest Austin, a young architect pointed out a house that his firm, reputedly one of the better ones in the city, had designed. It was a zero-lot-line house —because the developer had insisted on applying that planning concept. But zero-lot-line development doesn't suit land that falls away rapidly; it's best attuned to subdivisions where the small outdoor areas are relatively flat. In fact, the architects had to design outdoor decks to supply the requisite levelness that nature had provided so prodigiously in most of Texas but had neglected in the hill country. In all, it was a house that didn't make sense, set in a landscape that had been trampled. If blame is to be meted out, it could be apportioned broadly: to the developer who operated as if this were still the 1950s, indifferent to the integrity of the land; to the architects who knew that what was being planned was inappropriate but didn't want to lose a commission; to government officials whose high standards of public "improvement" have heightened the likelihood that the character of land will be lost; and to the residents who purchase such houses without protest.

What makes the situation so appalling is that just a few miles away sits West Lake Hills, a steep, wooded district that has been developing for the past thirty years without giving up the things that made it so attractive initially. Drive the winding roads of West Lake Hills and you find an environment where roadrunners scurry across the narrow pavement and where deer can be seen browsing in the woods near brooks, mountain laurel, and outcroppings of limestone. Trees — cedar and live oaks especially — create a canopy of continuous shade for the houses. Admittedly, the extent of public improvement in West Lake Hills is smaller. The streets are more abrupt in their twists and turns and ups and downs than civil engineering practice usually considers desirable. They're also narrower. When rain reaches the roads, it runs off naturally, meaning that once in a while a low spot in the road becomes impassable and people briefly have to drive a different route. Instead of municipal sewage-treatment systems, homeowners rely on septic tanks.

The cost of land makes it impossible for every
town to use the large lots of West Lake Hills as

TOP
A long, curving wall of the Lange house by Fred Linn Osmon in Carefree, Arizona, embraces a swimming pool in much the same fashion that older houses embraced fountains.
ABOVE
Another of Osmon's "desert boats," riding above its prickly landscape.
OPPOSITE
In the Rabinowitz house, Osmon combines sensuous curves with unobstructed vistas of the desert and Black Mountain.

a model; houses in the area, a 10- to 15-minute drive from downtown Austin, sit on lots of an acre or more. But it should be remembered that land is more affordable when expensive road, water, sewer, and land-regrading projects are kept to a minimum. There's been little cutting,

grading, filling, and bridge building in West Lake Hills; the land has not been flattened or reconfigured. All those economies have helped people to afford to live on what are, by today's standards, very large lots, in harmony with the land. After a long period of development, West Lake Hills retains its semirural atmosphere. People there still feel as if they're living in the woods. This is the approach that more municipalities would be wise to emulate, for one of the abiding ironies of American homebuilding is that as the standards of public "improvement" go higher, the livability of many of the settings declines.

A rigorously geometric house by Florida architect Carl Abbott wraps around part of its grounds (top), *and at the same time captures long views toward Sarasota's Lido Bay.*

Coming to terms with a setting is harder than is sometimes thought. A good house manages to do two different things with the land and with the other aspects of its setting. First, it takes the setting and makes it usable, forming interior and exterior spaces that are pleasing to inhabit. Second, and considerably more difficult, it enriches the larger environment. Some houses succeed at only one of these objectives — usually the former, as it is easier to design a house to fit the occupants' living patterns than to organize it so that it responds artfully to the surrounding landscape. Builders and homeowners have a ready stock of tools and arrangements for making outdoor areas usable and enjoyable: decks, patios, porches, atriums, courtyards, walls, fences, and so on. It's a relatively simple thing to apply mechanisms like these to yet another house or group of houses. But designing and building houses that somehow enhance the greater environment is a more complicated undertaking, requiring sensitive judgment about what makes the particular setting appealing and how the house can relate to that setting's critical attributes.

There's a great variety of approaches from which to choose, as should be evident by now. The goal is not necessarily to make the house blend quietly into the background. There are beautiful houses that stand out from their surroundings — and even not-so-beautiful houses, like the "little boxes" on the hillsides south of San Francisco, that, by standing out, give their setting an undeniable charm. In particular, some Modernist houses hover above the landscape — pristine sculptural objects with the ground below acting as the stage on which the architectural performance takes place. The surroundings are clearly subservient, and yet the combination of house and land makes a compelling composition. The magic lies in the contrast. Only a house with some special quality can make such a contrast work; the building has to be worthy of the exaltation. But if dozens of other houses of competing designs rise from their own stages nearby, the virtuoso performance falls victim to chaos.

More often, a house succeeds by establishing some kind of harmonious involvement with its grounds. In the Arizona desert, architect Fred Linn Osmon designs houses with desert colors — lots of tan tones — and puts walls high enough around the patios to deter jack rabbits and rattlesnakes. Then he lets the natural vegetation of the region lap up against the edges of these dwellings, which he sees as being "desert boats," riding just slightly above the landscape. On the Gulf Coast of Florida, Sarasota architect Carl Abbott makes his houses sharply geometric, with an abundance of glass so that residents can enjoy the magnificent vistas to the fullest, and he sometimes sends elements of the houses gliding smoothly out into the surrounding environment. For instance, a wooden walkway that starts along a living room wall extends outward until it hovers above the surface of a sparkling blue bay; a deck evolves into a dock. Other architects stake out prominent hillside locations for the houses they design but take pains to accentuate the contours of the terrain so that the house form and the land form reinforce each other.

With most houses, the challenge is to discover how to create patterns that are consistent with the neighboring homes and with the existing network of streets and public areas. This is the hardest task of all, particularly in a society that prizes individualism. What's needed is an equilibrium between variety and similarity so that the settings of American houses can achieve their potential. Certainly it's within the realm of the possible. From Boca del Mar to Omaha to San Francisco, new houses demonstrate attractive suggestions as to how to proceed.

Chapter Two

The Forms and Features of New Houses

Embellished surfaces of the Hal Box house in Austin, Texas, culminate in an octagonal dome 32 feet high above the center of the living room.

ABOVE
Pitched ceiling lends a sense of spaciousness to a bed-
room by Fisher-Friedman (left). Sculpted ceiling in house
by Carefree, Arizona, architect Fred Osmon (right).
OPPOSITE
The spare, yet grand interior of a townhouse by William F.
Stern on Albans Street in Houston.
OVERLEAF
A house in Sun City West, Arizona.

63

What is as beloved among architects as a grid? Modernists used it, Postmodernists play with it, and on these little houses on Germania Street in San Francisco, Donald MacDonald employs it as an eye-popping pattern in wood. The underlying form of the houses—that of a peak-roofed cottage—has also been used by MacDonald at several other San Francisco locations, but with more conventional clapboard siding.

Interior of an 11-unit apartment building MacDonald designed on Clay Street in San Francisco.

In the Foster house, the dining area is at one end of the ground floor of a 2½-story living area, which accommodates a library and study in the second story and catches diffuse light from dormer windows above.

68

On a wooded hillside overlooking the Potomac River in McLean, Virginia, stands the Foster house—a luxurious, 6,000-square-foot residence built in 1981 for a real estate executive, his wife, and their two children. The Fosters had originally been searching for an old farmhouse to buy and renovate, and when they couldn't find one in a location they liked, they asked Hartman-Cox Architects, in Washington, D.C., to design a new house that would evoke the feeling of a comfortable old home in the northern Virginia countryside. The new house rises two and a half stories, like many of the region's nineteenth-century farmhouses. Its walls of yellow, traditional-looking horizontal siding are interspersed at regular intervals with long, narrow four-over-four windows painted white—the kind of double-hung windows that suggest the style of the nineteenth century.

More than three times the size of the average new American house—much larger, too, than the typical dwelling of a century ago—the Foster house is an oversize but otherwise almost perfect embodiment of the aspirations that millions of Americans have for their homes in the 1980s. The Fosters' is a house that we'll return to often because it illustrates so many current attitudes toward residential design. One of the most striking things about this house is that, like many being built today, it's at ease using elements from the past. Its bulk is broken into three staggered segments whose proportions and detailing recall a time when what is now suburban northern Virginia was mainly farmland. Its gable roofs are surfaced in orange metal, a material routinely used on unpretentious rural dwellings. "Snowbirds"—little metal creatures that were traditionally used to prevent sheets of snow from cascading off of the roof and onto the heads of unsuspecting people below—deco-rate the lower roof edges, while dormers with crisp, white-painted, pointed-arch windows punctuate the roof at middle height.

Inside, though, a surprise awaits you: the dormers aren't part of an attic or a third-floor bedroom, as they would be in a nineteenth-century house. Instead, they and the pitched ceiling are the airy top of an open interior that stretches 29 feet from the house's ground floor to its peak. What the dormers actually do—besides accentuate the farmhouse esthetic of the exterior—is bring a soft, diffused sunlight into the library and study (occupying continuous balconies along the perimeter of the second floor) and let light penetrate down to the first-floor living room.

━━━

This blending of traditionalism and of more open, dramatic, and modern interior design is increasingly evident in American houses for various reasons. The exteriors may adopt a traditional appearance out of personal taste or because of a sense of social obligation. In the West Village historic district in Buffalo, New York, new brick-veneered houses have pitched roofs with dormers to help them blend in with nearby houses that were built in the late nineteenth century. Yet on the interior, as in the Foster house, most of the dormers let light penetrate from the top of the house all the way down to the ground floor. The flat ceilings and walls that divided older houses into a collection of self-contained rooms are giving way to looser, more expansive houseplans.

It was in the period after the Second World War that openness became particularly popular in American houses, and the legacy of that openness is now being assimilated into homes of many different styles. Often, today's floor plans elaborate on the postwar tendency toward dissolving the barriers between the kitchen and the dining room, between the dining room and the living room, or between the kitchen and the family room. Though large homes may have a formal dining room, in many houses it's common for the dining room to be separated from the living room by only a half-wall or a slight change of level. The dining area may be set apart from the kitchen by a line of base cabinets and upper cabinets, allowing a pass-through area at waist height. In some houses, the family room and the kitchen are fully or partly joined.

At first, the opening up of American houses was predominantly horizontal—a matter of dispensing with unnecessary partition walls. More recently, however, the desire for unobstructed, generous interiors has been affecting vertical dimensions as well. It's now common, even in regions as architecturally conservative as the Midwest, to see the interior expanding upward. In many American houses, the main living area has a high, sloped ceiling and more than one level. Lofts—sometimes overlooking the living room, sometimes a bedroom or study—have become popular. Stairways to the second floor, rather than being enclosed, often command a view of the main living area. Occasionally—especially in California—a second-floor walkway that connects a stairway to the bedroom area will extend dramatically above the forward portion of the living room. Townhouses sometimes have skylights in the roof and an opening in an upper-level floor that let natural light reach the core of the house. Traditional rectangular room arrangements will never disappear —a center-hall Colonial, with living room to one side and dining room and kitchen to the other, remains the most popular houseplan in much of the South—but a looser structuring of interiors is gaining acceptance. The era of boxy interiors is being supplanted by a new age of often-exciting interior vistas.

Sometimes structural elements that support the ceiling and roof can enliven the entire house. In southern Connecticut, William Grover of the architectural firm of Centerbrook designed a house whose roof rises, tentlike, toward the center. In the living room, where the roof reaches its peak, the exposed rafters are painted white and decorated with cheerful yellow crescents— one of the owners calls them her "smiles." The house isn't especially large—2,050 square feet, enough for a retired couple with occasional visitors—but because the roof slope and the rafters extend throughout the house, it feels bigger. You can stand in the kitchen, a bathroom, or a bedroom and be visually reminded that each room is part of a larger entity. Even painting the rafters different colors in different rooms doesn't diminish the pleasing sense that the house is a well-integrated whole.

Some houses, of course, continue to be divided into distinctly separate rooms. Yet these rooms, too, can use height to project a sense of spaciousness. Some rooms have a ceiling that slopes in one direction. Some have a ceiling with two slopes—often a cathedral ceiling. Others have ceilings that combine more than one shape. In Atlanta, a conservative bastion where houses often use Georgian styling on the outside and elaborate moldings on their interior walls, builders avoid boxiness by making "tray ceilings," which start horizontally at the perimeter of the room, rise at an angle for 2 or 3 feet, and then continue flat across the room's center. Most builders use a few varieties of dramatic "volume ceilings," as they're called, in major social areas such as the living room and dining room and in the master bedroom. If a tray ceiling is used in one room, another kind of volume ceiling may be used elsewhere in the house.

But this isn't the only approach. A few architects, such as Fred Linn Osmon, in Carefree,

With the aid of a brick fireplace (above), *and of inexpensive gypsumboard* (left), *interior areas in these two houses are defined without being closed off. In the house at left, the sense of volume is further enhanced by the balcony cutout.*

Arizona, have turned ceilings into free-form sculpted shapes—curving, stepping up, achieving a looseness that's unexpected and enchanting in a ceiling. Nearly everyone involved in houses—builders, architects, owners, tenants—has become increasingly aware of the wide range of possibilities. An interesting ceiling can lift the spirit at the same time that it lifts the eyes.

The real test of the designer's talent is whether he or she can strike a comfortable balance between drama and human scale. The Foster house, for all its openness, never lets the effects get out of control. The great vertical opening avoids the starkness of many contemporary houses, which, in their quest for excitement, place a clerestory window far at the top of the living room and leave the ground-floor inhabitants feeling as if they're sitting at the bottom of a chasm. Much of the Foster house's living room sits under a calmly horizontal 9-foot ceiling. Only the center portion of the ceiling is cut out, and, in looking up, you see the handsome balusters and railings of the second-floor balcony. The traditional detailing helps to establish a pleasant domestic atmosphere.

The desire for an attractive, generous openness is making a big impact on certain rooms, especially the kitchen. Early in this century, the American kitchen was hidden in an inconspicuous back corner, and everybody except family members, close friends, or servants was kept out of it. The days of the concealed kitchen, though, are long gone. Some forty years ago, the kitchen began moving toward a more prominent position, and now it's becoming the glamour spot of many upper-income houses. If kitchens once were little more than sanitary and functional, they are now alluring. Some people are designing them large and luxurious enough to be used for entertaining. "It's no longer a taboo to watch the food preparation," says architect Bernard M. Wharton of Shope Reno Wharton in Greenwich, Connecticut. When guests come over for dinner, they often join their hosts in the kitchen while the meal is being put together. Melanie Taylor of Orr & Taylor Architecture and Gardens in New Haven, Connecticut, frequently provides a counter or "something informal that people can lean up against at some distance from the work area, so that they feel they're a part of things, and yet they don't get spattered or get in the way of the cook." The solution at the Foster house lay in placing the sink, cooking surfaces, and food-preparation areas in a galley-style work center, separated from the kitchen's sitting area only by a counter a little less than chest-high.

The array of appliances in today's kitchens is so extensive that some kitchen specialists accuse their clients of having "mixer envy." So many small appliances compete for space in well-equipped kitchens that some people have inserted "appliance garages" under the wall cabinets. (These are supposed to make the kitchen neat and tidy, which is usually an illusion; some variation on Murphy's law ensures that the quantity of kitchen clutter invariably expands to fill all the available counter space.) Appliances keep proliferating. Dishwashers have become standard items, and microwave ovens are nearly always expected in new kitchens. As food and kitchens have become increasingly important adjuncts of fashion, restaurant-quality ranges and restaurant-quality refrigerators have also made their way into chic kitchens.

The question is: what should be exposed and what should blend inconspicuously into the background? Builders have become adept at placing counters so that people in an adjoining family room or dining area can look into the

Kitchens

*The kitchen need not be a predictable rectangular box. It
can incorporate a curved built-in seating area, as in the
design by Moore Ruble Yudell* (left), *or curves in the
ceiling, as in a house by Howard Barnstone* (below).
OVERLEAF
*Marble counters and a classical-inspired booth in
architect Bernard M. Wharton's kitchen* (page 74), *and
Peter Shire's splashy use of ColorCore* (page 75).

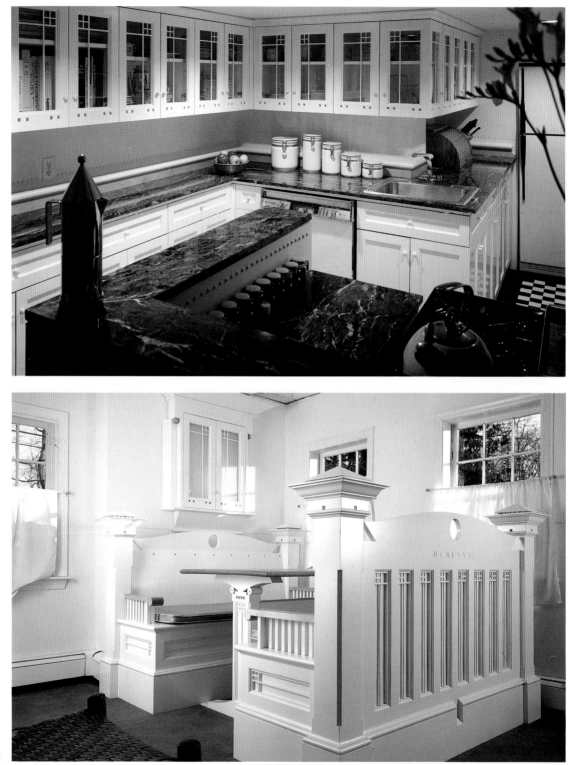

Dining areas open to the kitchen in designs by William F. Stern (left) *and J. P. Chadwick Floyd* (above).

OVERLEAF

Snack counter in Fisher-Friedman's "New American Home" for the National Association of Home Builders (page 78), *and a greenhouse-style extension in a kitchen by Kenneth Schroeder & Associates* (page 79).

77

ABOVE
A curving half-wall of glass block in a kitchen by Duo Dickinson of Mackall & Dickinson.

RIGHT
Island counter and skylit seating in Norman Jaffe's Hillman house in East Hampton, New York.

OPPOSITE
Center islands in two Maine Post & Beam kitchens, combining work area, dining surface, and under-counter storage.

kitchen without seeing dirty dishes. Generally, however, only architect-designed kitchens have succeeded in playing down the big appliances that unwittingly turn the typical kitchen into a hard-surfaced exhibit of domestic technology. In the Foster house, people in the kitchen's sitting area can see upper portions of the refrigerator, for instance, but its doors have been paneled to blend in with old-fashioned-looking surroundings of a kitchen furnished with country antiques. The paneling makes the kitchen seem more relaxed—an effect reinforced by a display of Mrs. Foster's pottery on shelves high on the wall above the food-preparation area. In a mass-produced house, the wall might have been covered with cabinets, but the Foster house, like many architect-designed houses, has ample storage out of sight—just around the corner in a pantry. Some designers, such as Louis Mackall of Breakfast Woodworks in Branford, Connecticut, encourage their customers to have pantries in part because they cost considerably less than cabinets; the only component of the pantry that needs a high-quality finish is the door.

Cabinets today range from the sleek look popularized by European manufacturers to traditional designs with a more three-dimensional character. The Europeans captured Americans' attention with cabinets that have doors smoothly butted up against one another, with no exposed hinges or visible frames. Drawer-pulls in European-style cabinetry are often just simple recesses. Countertops in most of today's houses continue to be covered in plastic laminates, but there is a growing number of alternative synthetics, from Formica Corporation's ColorCore —a solid material with color throughout, rather than a veneer—to DuPont's Corian, a solid, nonporous acrylic-based material with an opalescent glow. Corian and competing products

like Avonite and Formica Brand 2000X can be sawn, drilled, and routed, giving their edges a sculpted appearance. Inlays of wood, metal, or other materials can decorate the edges or tops of the counters.

In California and parts of the Southwest, tile countertops have become increasingly popular. And in upper-income kitchens across the country, marble and granite have emerged as favored materials for countertops. Marble is especially good for making pastry; the stone stays cool and smooth, so dough can be rolled on it with ease. In kitchens not blessed with such princely budgets, a small section of marble may be inserted into a countertop of plastic laminate. One advantage of marble, granite, and ceramic tile is their ability to absorb the heat of pots taken off the stove and placed directly on the counter. The main reason for the arrival of stone, however, is its look and feel; marble and granite are handsome natural materials that give a kitchen an aura of opulence. People are increasingly looking for the kitchen to have an inviting texture and atmosphere. Special touches are what count.

Kitchens now come in all sorts of shapes, although the most practical ones adhere to the "work-triangle" approach to planning, in which the refrigerator, sink, and cooktop are convenient to one another. Many people want an island work counter, which, depending on its size and the owners' preferences, may contain a sink or a downdraft grill. The island counter is so popular that Kaufman-Meeks, a Houston firm that designs houses for builders across much of the nation, even tries to provide a small island (with a countertop, but no sink or cooktop, on a base cabinet about two feet square) in houses intended for first-time homebuyers.

Largely because of the proliferation of two-career households — more than half the married women in the United States now earn paychecks — some kitchens are being designed with two work stations so that when husband and wife get home, they can both help to prepare the evening meal. Two distinct work areas, each with its own sink, enable two people to keep out of each other's way while going about their kitchen tasks. Readying meat for cooking may take place at one sink area close to a microwave oven. The other sink area, used for jobs such as making salads, may be near the refrigerator. The cooking surface may be placed between the two. The two work triangles overlap.

Designers are paying more attention to the informal eating area, usually labeled a "breakfast area" on houseplans. Instead of being just a place for a table along a wall, it's increasingly an area that's upgraded with special features such as skylights. Some kitchens also have built-in desks. Kitchens and their informal eating areas often open up to the family room or "great room," where the TV set, stereo equipment, and fireplace are most likely located. A few houses have a special media room for large-screen viewing and other electronic features, which otherwise tend to dominate a family room. The formally decorated living room continues on, but most of the time it stands empty. Millions of people regard the living room like a good suit: they need to have one, but they use it only on special occasions. Family members and close friends gravitate to the family room or kitchen. A lot of people are tempted to eliminate the living room altogether but don't quite have the nerve. Instead, the living room today is frequently reduced in size, some of its space shifted to the family room–kitchen area where everyday activities concentrate.

The other major focal point of today's home design is the master bedroom suite, which in the past decade has grown in both size and lavishness. Increasingly, the master bedroom suite is a world unto itself, placed at some distance from the bedrooms of children. As floor plans have opened up, making each room in the public part of the house more accessible to the others, adults have had to go somewhere to escape; the psychology of the master bedroom suite is even intimated with a new term: the "master retreat." In a two-story house, the master retreat is often situated on the ground floor, a convenient location especially for couples whose children have reached college age or older. When no children are staying at home, the second floor can basically be closed down. On the first floor, it's easier, too, to provide a private deck or patio — sometimes secluded behind fences or walls — for the master bedroom. There may also be a sitting area inside, at one end of the bedroom. But almost certainly, in a house of more than moderate size, the master bedroom will have at least one walk-in closet. Even mobile homes today sometimes come equipped with walk-in closets. In some houses, there are separate his-and-hers walk-in closets — not necessarily identical in size, since the woman usually has a larger wardrobe.

More important than closet space is the spaciousness and luxury of the master bathroom. The old small, Spartan bathroom — functional, but not much more — has given way to bathrooms that are expansive and extravagantly detailed. In upper price ranges, opulent materials have appeared. Because of advances in stone-fabricating technology, marble can now be cut into tiles well under half an inch thick; these tiles are easier to work with and less expensive than slabs of marble. They're being used in **83**

*The master bathroom has evolved into one of the most
sumptuous parts of the house, incorporating such
features as glass block walls, skylights, and platform
baths. The bath on the facing page* (bottom) *commands
a view of a private walled garden.*

many affluent bathrooms—often on walls and as surrounds for tubs. When the bathtub is treated this grandly—and often even when it's not—the tub is entirely separate from the shower stall; the combination tub and shower has now been relegated to smaller or less stylish houses. Often the tub is a whirlpool bath, and it may be designed to accommodate more than one person. It may also be part of an elegant platform. Anyone who's been to a recent National Association of Home Builders convention knows that it's usually the plumbing manufacturers who end up stealing the show with extravagant displays of one- to four-person whirlpool baths and sculpted sinks, toilets, and bidets. The bathroom is getting a huge amount of design attention and investment; in older houses that are being remodeled, the bathroom may consume the space once occupied by a bedroom.

Skylights illuminate hundreds of thousands of today's bathrooms, and many designers place the tub where it commands a view outdoors. Better-insulating windows, introduced in the past few years, can keep a bathtub next to glass from becoming quite as uncomfortable during a bitter Northern winter as would have been true in the past. Even so, the bath-with-a-view is really best suited to mild climates, although it has been adopted without much thought by some builders in cold regions. It's astonishing to walk through model homes in different parts of the country and see features that the builder apparently picked up from national magazines or conventions and applied without taking into account the local climate or vistas. In Florida, where nearly all the houses are one-story, a bath looking out onto a lush private garden is delightful. But you can go into two-story suburbs outside Chicago and find the same tub in the same position, now in a second-floor location next to a cold window that delivers a medi-

ocre view and can be seen by neighbors. A lot of window blinds are going to be sold before this decade is out.

Today's houses make it somewhat easier for husband and wife to get up and get ready for work at the same time in the morning. They subdivide the master bathroom—placing the toilet, for instance, in a separate cubicle. (Atlanta builder J. David Chatham augments the toilet cubicle with bookshelves since, he says, it "becomes the reading room.") Double-bowl vanities are popular throughout the country, but for those who prefer privacy, it's more sensible to put sinks or vanities in separate compartments. Some houses have one sink in the bathroom and a second sink in a vanity that's in a dressing area nearer the bedroom. Occasionally, to give this make-up area a more spacious feeling, it's open to the bedroom.

Until now, many people seem to have become infatuated with the idea of making their bathroom bigger and more luxurious, but what we may see in the future is more clever and functional compartmentalization of the space. In the Connecticut house designed by William Grover, for example, the husband and wife have separate bedrooms, as is common among retirement-age couples. The bedrooms are in two corners of the house, and in between, along an exterior wall, is a linear bathroom that consists of three compartments, which can be opened to make one long room or closed off into private segments. Adjacent to the man's bedroom is a compartment containing a sink and toilet. Adjacent to the woman's bedroom is a much larger compartment with sink, toilet, bidet, and bathtub. The middle compartment houses a shower stall and counter space. There's also a linear dressing area along an inside wall, running from the main door of one bedroom to the main door of the other, so the bathroom is not the only corridor to connect the bedrooms.

The variety of other features being incorporated into today's master bedroom suites is enormous. Some have platform beds, fireplaces, exercise areas, and handsome built-in cabinets for TV sets. Some have an adjoining study, removed from the distractions of the rest of the house. And for the truly rich of Texas, who inhabit houses of several thousand square feet, yet another luxury has appeared: a master suite with its own private kitchen where the servants do not intrude. This is the ultimate aim of the master bedroom suite: all the best a home has to offer, gathered close to the bed. A house within a house.

A similarly strong trend toward elaboration is taking place on the outsides of houses. Many designers have rebeled against the spare and the simple. Where houses once put all their rooms under one continuous roof, the tendency now is to break the roof into a complex collection of shapes. A high hip roof sends forth two or three smaller hip roofs closer to ground level. Small gables branch from large gables. Dormers pop up from roofs, and bay windows protrude from walls. Greenhouses sprout on the sunny side of the house, and "greenhouse windows" project from kitchens and bathrooms, letting in more light and enabling the house to be decorated with plants.

The tendency toward elaboration has produced some fascinating houses—buildings that can't be understood at a glance, buildings that reward continued looking. In the Foster house, the staggered arrangement of the house made it easier to separate the house into three main zones—the living room, dining room, library, and study in the center; the children's bedrooms and a pottery studio at one end; and the kitchen, with master bedroom suite above, at the other

end. The gables and dormers form a functional and visually effective composition.

But complexity today often gets out of control. It has produced streets so jumpy with restless walls and active roofs that it's hard to decide exactly what to focus on; all the architectural components are calling, almost brawling, for attention. Quite a few designers, especially those who work for mass-production home-builders, have acted on the assumption that the more elaborate the façade, the better it is—which can be disproven with a single glance down some of the polystyrene-Tudor streets scattered across America. What's needed is more attention to whether the shapes serve meaningful purposes and how they add up to a coherent composition. Stronger organization is needed so that small features coordinate with larger focal points. If houses once erred on the side of austerity, they now go astray by turning complexity into confusion.

What's being sought, it's clear, is a full, rich, individualized composition—a worthy objective in itself. This quest is nowhere more evident than in today's small houses. Small dwellings are being designed so that they feel more important than their size alone would suggest. One of the keys to dignifying the small house is the orchestration of an interesting procession from street to door. A short, straight walkway may be the cheapest and most direct path, but rarely is it the most charming. Many designers have learned to put the main entrance at the side of the house, partway back, so that you get away from the street and pass through a relatively private, generously landscaped environment that conveys a gracious sense of arrival. In a subdivision west of Houston developed by NPC Homebuilders and designed by Kaufman Meeks, two-bedroom, two-bath detached houses of 850

ABOVE
A layered, yet transparent entrance designed by Booth/Hansen & Associates helps bring light into a house whose narrow Chicago lot would otherwise result in a dark interior.

LEFT
The yearning for a romantic arrival occasionally breeds exercises in cuteness.

OPPOSITE
Separate stairs for each unit at Mission Verde in Camarillo, California, make this complex by Berkus Group Architects visually busy; but they also give each residence an entrance that seems less public and anonymous.

square feet sit on tiny lots, but the entrance path takes you through a lattice arch on the way to the door, so the houses avoid seeming overly Spartan. In addition, they have shutters, picket fences, and more than one gable on their roofs.

Sometimes, in trying to give the small house a magnetic personality, the designers sacrifice practical considerations. Inside one particular 850-square-foot house, you discover that one of the windows enhancing the house's street-side appeal is situated in a walk-in closet, exposing clothing to sun and making the compartment uncomfortably hot. The house's pleasant side entrance, with its romantic walk, actually positions guests so that, while waiting at the door, they stand next to the large window of the master bathroom. These are the sorts of trade-offs sometimes being made by designers who are intent on producing small houses on small lots and maximizing their charm.

Designing for emotional impact—which is what the architects of some small houses are doing—may pose an additional problem that's less readily apparent. It has to do with a person's reaction to a building not being fixed; the response changes with time, as the person becomes more familiar with the building. One of the joys of a good work of architecture is that you gradually recognize more of its logic and discover that the decisions about the building's form and composition were based on substantial, interlocking reasons. Conversely, one of the things that makes a bad work of architecture disturbing is the discovery that design decisions were based on a flimsy or, even worse, demeaning rationale.

The trouble with some initially charming small houses is that the closer you look, the more you recognize their shallowness. Design elements whose sole purpose is to appeal to sentiment are especially vulnerable to a rude

reappraisal. What will a homeowner feel about a lattice arch after walking through it a thousand times? Unless the arch is part of some larger structure—such as a fence and gate that enhance security—or serves some auxiliary purpose, the homeowner may conclude that the device is intended to provoke an emotional response and nothing more. At that point, the owners may feel that the builder has sold them something useless; homeowners are a skeptical breed, and their fears that they've been taken in need to be allayed, lest they become disenchanted. Some architectural emotion-enhancers —such as little roof extensions that are supposed to cast an air of charm across the entrance path and that aren't adaptable to porches or patios—may well give homeowners a dawning awareness that they've been manipulated by the builder. And this may result in their not only disliking the builder but also resenting their own vulnerability and becoming dissatisfied with the house. The emotions that tie people to their houses ought not to be trifled with.

This is not to suggest that a cold, purely functional approach to building is preferable. On the contrary, a house should be much more than a mechanical arrangement of rooms; it should be able to move us as well as accommodate our physical needs. But if architectural and decorative elements are going to be used to make a house picturesque, those features should have some additional justification based on structural concerns, function, or other needs. If all of this sounds a bit like a sermon, keep in mind that for a long while many American houses were bare-bones affairs, at least on the outside. It's refreshing to see architects and builders now producing houses that possess feeling, and it would be a shame to see the use of picturesque elements become so egregiously maudlin as to generate a counterreaction back toward drabness and sterility. Right now, there's a danger that excesses of manipulative romanticism will spark just such a movement toward dwellings that are clean-looking but numb.

The techniques that bestow importance and allure on small detached houses also add appeal to attached housing. Shared internal corridors are disappearing from many rental complexes. Instead, each unit opens directly onto the outdoors, and, in many cases, it has a walkway that, at least within a few feet of the door, is not shared with neighbors. At Mission Verde, a condominium complex designed by Berkus Group Architects in Camarillo, California, some of the condos are 1-bedroom, 844-square-foot units with a circulation system that directs the resident up a private outdoor stairway. Not only is the stairway private, but an arched entryway further heightens the pleasure of arrival. On the exterior of this complex, designed in a simplified Spanish Colonial style, there are decks with walls high enough to shield residents from prying eyes; someone can sunbathe on a second-floor deck without being seen by neighbors.

The goal, says Barry Berkus, is to provide housing that is "exciting, flexible and stimulating enough—not just a filing cabinet, a cube." That objective becomes abundantly clear on the inside of many of today's small houses, whether attached or detached. Often some of the walls are placed at other than right angles to avoid boxiness and to give residents long diagonal views through the interior. By placing windows in the corners and at the end of sight lines, occupants are invited to look beyond the interior, enhancing the sense of spaciousness. Halls are virtually eliminated. Stairways are open, to prevent losing any sense of volume in the areas they pass through. Mirrors, if not overused, magnify the impression of spaciousness.

The openness that adds drama to houses of ordinary size is especially important in making small units attractive. Some 600-square-foot condominium units designed by Mithun Bowman Emrich Group, of Bellevue, Washington, are laid out so that a partition wall containing a fireplace separates the bedroom from the living area without dividing them into entirely separate rooms. The partition extends from floor to ceiling in the center of the apartment, yet leaves openings along the perimeter. On tiny lots in San Francisco, architect Donald MacDonald has designed 2-story cottages measuring 20 by 20 feet, with a bathroom and bedrooms on the ground floor and living, dining, and kitchen areas on the second—often under a loft and under skylights set into a sloping roof. A sloped ceiling can make a modest living room much more comfortable. A balconied second story can even give it some excitement. Small units are particularly well suited for taking attic space, which might have gone unused, and adding it to the space below, creating high, spectacular interiors.

No design technique is without disadvantages, and soaring interiors are no exception. It's not uncommon for windows to be placed so far out of reach that a long ladder or a special extension tool is needed just to open and close them. The large sweep of walls also presents a challenge to interior decorating. Builders typically attempt to make the tall interiors softer and more intimate in scale by embellishing the

OVERLEAF

A cottage at Seaside, Florida (above), *by Orr & Taylor, and its symmetrical floor plan. Also, sitting areas by the windows in a William F. Stern house and in the predominantly open interior of Booth/Hansen's Chicago house.*

Outdoor shower

Bedroom

Bedroom

Living/dining room

Kitchen

Porch

walls with ledges on which baskets, plants, or other decorations can be displayed. The question of whether dramatically open interiors exceed a comfortably human scale more often applies in a full-size detached house, but designers increasingly are finding ways to keep such spaces from feeling overwhelming. Small bays and alcoves provide cozy places to sit. Color schemes have softened; instead of the unvarying white of Modernist houses, grays and pastels have come into favor, setting one room apart from another. Even in houses that are predominantly open, there's a greater attempt now to differentiate between one area and another. Traditional elements such as moldings, balusters, and columns give the house a more familiar, domestic character. One particularly strong example of the esthetic shift is windows. Where houses once used large sheets of glass to make the division between indoors and out almost disappear, the preference is now for windows divided into small panes, which are more enclosing and cozier to sit beside.

The shift toward a more intimate scale has made it easier to fit old or traditional furnishings into today's houses. "Many people in the past were buying for their homes the same furniture that could have sat in a corporate lobby," Melanie Taylor observes. Breuer chairs, long sectional couches, chrome and glass coffee tables—these were Modernist favorites. Now, with a different esthetic, such furnishings as wing chairs, mahogany side tables, and chintz-covered sofas have found a place in some of today's new homes. Small houses that Orr & Taylor designed in the new town of Seaside, in the Florida Panhandle, have a cozy, old-fashioned atmosphere, even though the rooms generally aren't entirely separated from one another.

94 In small housing units intended for sale to owner-occupants, builders are increasingly trying to offer the features associated with detached houses. In the San Jose area of northern California, Barratt Ltd. has introduced condominium units as small as 432 and 486 square feet. These are simple one-story apartments on the ground floor or one level up. They are about as compact as owner-occupied housing ever gets outside America's densest cities, and yet Barratt, after some initial experimentation, saw to it that a garage and a patio or deck were provided for each owner, that the closets and bathrooms assumed a reasonably normal size, and that washers and dryers were installed in each unit rather than in a shared laundry room.

Small housing units have received attention in recent years from all segments of the homebuilding industry, especially in regions, such as California, where housing costs have been rising fastest. Although condominium units of less than 550 square feet are rare and will probably remain so, there will likely be considerable construction of units ranging from 550 or 600 square feet to a little over 1,000 square feet. It's in this segment of homebuilding that some of the most imaginative work is being done.

To some extent, size matters less than amenities. Even though new houses are no longer growing significantly—the median size of detached single-family homes has hovered near 1,600 square feet for more than a decade—their range of features keeps expanding. Many of the amenities have to do with mechanical or electronic devices rather than with architecture. Wet bars, trash compactors, ice-cube dispensing refrigerators, burglar alarms—these are among the features increasingly in demand. There now are systems like General Electric's "Home Minder" that enable people to control lights, appliances, and furnaces from any room in the house—or by pressing buttons on a telephone miles away. The system's series of control modules, many of which are plugged into the house's electrical sockets, also make it possible to instruct appliances and other household devices to operate at specified times.

The next step is to build houses in which this kind of amenity is provided by their basic electrical systems rather than supplied by an auxiliary product like Home Minder. If the "Smart House" venture administered by the National Association of Home Builders Research Foundation is successful, thousands of houses will soon be built with an integrated wiring system replacing the separate wires and cables now installed for appliances, phones, cable TV, security, and thermostats. This would not only enable people to program every device in the house—turning up the house's thermostat and turning on the oven to cook the evening meal while the owner is driving home, for instance —but it would also eliminate many electrical fires, electrocutions, and other accidents. A microchip in each device would tell the system how much electricity the device requires and whether the device is operating properly; only the appropriate amount of current would be supplied. If a baby stuck his finger in a socket, for example, no electricity would flow, since none was authorized by a microchip.

Since any Smart House device could operate in any outlet, you could have a stereo receiver in the living room provide music for speakers in the bedroom or basement—without running any additional wiring to those locations. The speakers could simply be plugged into the nearest sockets. The system could also compensate for people's disabilities. By programing the Smart House system to respond to voice commands, a blind person, for example, could find out which lights are on and could more easily run kitchen appliances and other devices that usually require manual control. For the wheelchair-bound—or for anyone—the lights could be instructed to come on as the person entered the room and to turn off after he left. The system could turn the heat on and off, depending on whether anyone was occupying the room. It could learn the household's patterns and use them to reduce energy consumption; if hot water is rarely used after 11 P.M., for instance, the system could stop heating water from then until whenever it's needed in the morning. All in all, Smart House technology—which was first demonstrated in a limited way for builders in 1986—could offer an appealing combination of safety, economy, and convenience.

Designing homes today is partly a matter of tailoring the housing to the needs of different kinds of residents. One of the groups receiving the most attention is older people. In 1960, when the first Sun City opened in Arizona, there were about 17 million Americans aged 65 or older, and they constituted just under 10 percent of the nation's population. By 1980, the elderly population had grown to 25.5 million, or 11 percent of the total, and by the end of the century it's expected to climb to 32 million, or 12 percent. In Florida alone, hundreds of developments cater to older people, setting a minimum age for residency, generally between fifty and the early sixties.

Most developments are able to meet their residents' needs with familiar kinds of housing. Townhouses, elevator apartment buildings, detached houses, or mobile homes comprise most of the housing in retirement complexes; the main attraction is the gathering together of people of one age group in a well-kept environment. In Florida, one of the most highly regarded of these developments is Hawthorne, at Leesburg, about 40 miles northwest of Orlando. Behind gates that are manned around the clock by a paid security force, 1,150 mobile homes sit along curving, well-planted drives, surrounded by lawns that are kept neat by a staff the residents' association hires. The 300-acre complex employs its own fire-and-emergency squad, which responds not only to telephone calls but also to emergency buttons installed in two locations in each home—in a bedroom area close to the bathroom, and in the living area. Hawthorne also has a 1,600-seat auditorium, a marina, library, chapel, putting green, heated pool, therapeutic pools, saunas, and covered shuffleboard courts, and it offers its residents more than 100 organized activities.

The mobile homes themselves, as might be expected, aren't much different from those that one can see elsewhere. In American housing as a whole, the custom is for people to select their housing from among the wide range of what's already known rather than to invent a new solution. Many retirees are uninterested in trying to impress others with the lavishness of their house; what they want is a comfortable house that's easy to maintain, and a mobile home meets this standard. Mobile homes don't require exterior painting, and even their interior walls need relatively little attention, since they're often sheathed in paneling instead of gypsumboard.

Genuinely innovative movements in architecture and planning are taking place in many other retirement housing complexes, especially in those designed for people who can no longer entirely look after themselves. For the oldest Americans, housing is coming to reflect finer gradations between self-sufficiency and dependence. A prime example of this trend is congregate living facilities that offer meals and **96** other support—now being developed throughout the country by for-profit companies and by nonprofit organizations.

Since 1982, Cardinal Industries, of Columbus, Ohio, has built 9 Cardinal Villages—retirement housing complexes of 73 to 150 units—in Ohio, Michigan, and Florida. The company applies a modular construction system that it has used since 1970 to build apartment complexes for the general population. Generally the apartments are 288, 576, or 864 square feet, with a screened private porch looking out on a grassy common area and with storage in an individual attic above each unit. A factory-built 12-by-24-foot module forms a studio apartment equipped with a kitchenette and full bathroom. Two modules placed side by side form a one-bedroom apartment containing a small kitchen, living area, bathroom, walk-in closet, and carpeted vanity–dressing area. Three modules form a two-bedroom, two-bath unit. All are ground-floor units, laid out along carpeted corridors like those in a conventional apartment complex. Where corridors intersect, a wider area has sometimes been furnished with couches and tables to encourage socializing with neighbors.

The typical Cardinal Village resident is a woman in her late seventies or eighties who sold her home after her husband died and who is using the equity to live in a complex offering more services than an ordinary apartment development would provide. Residents can have dinner each evening in a dining room that serves the entire complex. As currently designed, each Cardinal Village also has a craft room, library, a room for meetings and other

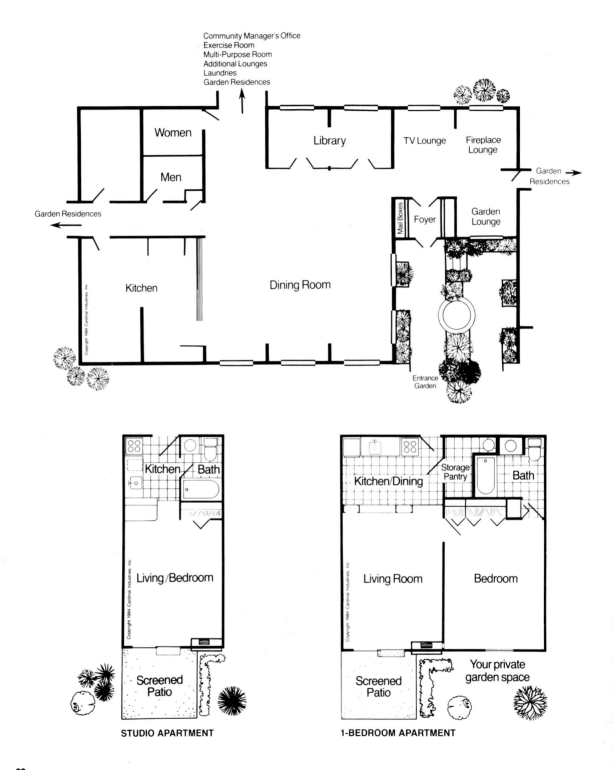

Community Manager's Office
Exercise Room
Multi-Purpose Room
Additional Lounges
Laundries
Garden Residences

Women

Men

Library

TV Lounge

Fireplace Lounge

Garden Residences

Garden Residences

Mail Boxes

Foyer

Garden Lounge

Kitchen

Dining Room

Entrance Garden

Kitchen

Bath

Living/Bedroom

Screened Patio

STUDIO APARTMENT

Kitchen/Dining

Storage Pantry

Bath

Living Room

Bedroom

Screened Patio

Your private garden space

1-BEDROOM APARTMENT

98   *Floor plans of common areas and of studio and one-bedroom apartments at Cardinal Village.*

activities, a beauty shop, laundry facilities, exercise room with a hot tub, a lounge, picnic areas, and a private dining room where a resident may entertain up to a dozen guests. Everything is on one level, behind security doors. Cardinal Villages aren't nursing homes, but some have a health counselor who attends to residents' welfare.

A Cardinal Village essentially is a rambling complex made up of the same modules that Cardinal Industries uses to build detached houses, small-town apartment complexes, and its chain of Knights Inn motels, except that common facilities have been added. By contrast, in Massachusetts, the state Executive Office of Communities and Development has organized a series of congregate living facilities that were designed by architects backed by research teams. Some of these complexes are far smaller than Cardinal Villages. At Eldridge House, in Hyannis, accommodations for twenty elderly people who cannot live entirely independently but who do not need nursing care were designed by a team made up of KJA Architects of Cambridge, Building Diagnostics Inc. of Boston, and Donham & Sweeney Architects of Boston.

The designers started with a 2,000-square-foot wood-frame house that had been built for a nineteenth-century sea captain, Clarence Eldridge, and added 8,500 square feet of harmonious new construction, distinguished on the exterior by a long front porch and old-fashioned gables and dormers. As a result of research that included questioning prospective residents about their preferences, the designers decided to provide several shared living areas— front and back parlors in the old portion of the house, a sitting room near a vehicle drop-off area, a large dining room, where one hot meal is provided daily, and the porch, which is fur-nished with tables and rocking chairs. The kitchen is also open to everyone's use.

A major issue was: which traditionally personal areas needed to be retained so that the residents can preserve their dignity and a degree of control over their lives? It was decided that each bathtub and shower would have to be shared by four people but that each resident would have a private toilet and wash basin. A second issue was how to provide privacy but at the same time enhance opportunities for spontaneous socializing. The designers dealt with this question by arranging each 270-square-foot apartment as two connected rectangles, the larger containing the bedroom, dressing area, and lavatory, the smaller containing a kitchenette and a door onto the building's public corridors. Consequently, the bedroom, often furnished more like a sitting room, is shielded from the glances of people in the corridors. The kitchenette is treated as an area from which residents can make contact with others when they wish. It is equipped with a window facing the corridor; the resident can open or close the curtains to encourage or discourage visitors. The door to the corridor is a Dutch door, making it still easier for residents to have a certain amount of privacy and yet strike up conversations with passers-by when they want to. Corridors are organized around a skylighted atrium that is open enough so that residents can see into public areas of the house before entering and either prepare for social encounters or avoid them. Areas outside each pair of units are arranged as recessed alcoves so that they can serve as a kind of front porch where people can sit when they want to be sociable.

Architecturally, Eldridge House is much more distinguished than a Cardinal Village, and sociologically it is more subtle. The building has been designed, with the help of sociologists, so that it has fine gradations from public to private space, presumably helping the residents obtain the precise degree of social contact they want at any given time. By comparison, at Cardinal Village a resident is either inside a private unit or out in the public realm, which may or may not be attractive for socializing. The couch-equipped corridor at a Cardinal Village, for instance, looks like a furnished afterthought—satisfactory in some instances but at other times forcing awkward conversations between the occupant of this *de facto* lounge and whoever unexpectedly comes down the hall.

Yet this is not to say that Cardinal Village is the wrong approach and Eldridge House is right. Eldridge House appears to be based on the idea that designing for social interaction is paramount when, in fact, many Americans, including some elderly people, may be just as interested, perhaps even more interested, in the size and completeness of the apartment itself. They may well value a full private bathroom, a bedroom separate from the living area, a screened porch, and enough space for their mementos and their own furniture more than a design that makes socializing easier.

This suggests that there's room for a variety of techniques in designing congregate apartments, or indeed any housing, for older people. Without question, there are going to be many more experiments and refinements. Cardinal Industries—though committed to construction based on 12-by-24-foot modules—has in 5 years modified its complexes considerably, deciding, for instance, that the developments need 120–150 apartments instead of the 73–83 units that were in the original complexes. And those who designed congregate housing in Massachusetts are continuing to refine their ideas. It turned out that Eldridge House residents decorated their interior porches to reflect their individual

tastes and they socialized with one another in some of the houses' common areas, but they didn't use the porches for sitting and talking with others, as had been hoped. In a more recent congregate facility that KJA Architects designed in Rochester, Massachusetts, there is a central outdoor courtyard instead of a central atrium, and the residents have real porches around it. These they enthusiastically use.

This is only a small sampling of what's being built for older Americans, but it indicates the vitality that's infusing the retirement housing field. In 1982, the United States had about 600 "life-care retirement communities," where residents typically were supplied with apartments, a health center, dining and community facilities, and other amenities, enabling them to shift from a more or less self-sufficient household unit to one supported by housekeeping, nutrition, and nursing services without moving out of the development. It's anticipated that by the end of the 1980s another 1,000 to 1,500 life-care communities will be in operation; the segment of the nation's population experiencing the fastest proportionate growth is people over the age of seventy-five.

Another group that is increasing rapidly is families in which both the father and the mother work outside the home. In 1960, both husband and wife in only 31 percent of the marriages in the United States held jobs outside the home. By 1981, according to an Insurance Information Institute report, this proportion had risen to 51 percent. Another study found that, in 1984, 48 percent of the mothers of American preschool children were employed. For millions of families the question is how to take care of their children during the work day. It's a question that developers and builders are just beginning to address. In 1984, Cenvill Development Corporation—which entered the housing field as the developer of four huge Century Villages in southern Florida for older people whose children had left home—started to build a subdivision for families with working parents. Centura Parc, in Coconut Creek, Florida, is made up of five "villages," each containing 164 townhouses and cluster homes. Within each village are two "Centers in the Parc," accessible both by street and by bicycle path. Each weekday, the centers care for children from three months to five years old. During the evenings and on weekends, some centers also offer babysitting for children from ages two through twelve.

In Los Angeles, Dolores Hayden, a housing historian, worked with architect Ena Dubnoff and the Los Angeles County Community Development Commission to design a forty-eight-unit residential project that's laid out to make child care easier. "The ruling concern," Hayden told the *New York Times,* "has been the working parents' need to have both institutional child care and informal supervision of children while doing such activities as cooking and laundry." Consequently, each apartment commands views of play areas. A large laundry and community room are adjacent to a playground. In addition, the complex also contains a child-care center that operates during the day and after school.

The child-care issue is especially acute for single-parent families. Some 10 million households are headed by women, nearly twice as many as in 1970. But although single-parent families are one of the fastest-growing segments of the population, housing rarely reflects this fact. In Hayward, California, Berkeley architect Mui Ho designed one of the few developments specifically oriented to the needs of this group. Sparks Way Commons, a limited-income complex constructed with government assistance, has organized its forty-five townhouses in clusters. Each group of five units faces a common courtyard, making it easier for parents to know and help one another. Instead of large private yards, which single parents have little time to maintain, much of the land has been consolidated into a grassy playfield for group sports. The development also has a "tot lot," a common laundry, and a community building, where child care can be provided in the future. Governmental regulations had called for parking spaces for 2.2 cars per unit, but the architect—seeing this as a poor use of scarce land—handled much of the parking area as a paved lot at the edge of the development, where part of it can double as basketball or volleyball courts for the children.

Quite a few single-parent families have dealt with their housing dilemma by moving back in with their parents or by sharing a house or apartment with others. Across the country, nearly 300 organizations help people—not necessarily single-parent families—arrange to share housing. For the newly divorced, joining with others to obtain living quarters can mean the difference between staying in middle-class surroundings and slipping into tougher neighborhoods with rougher schools. North of San Francisco in affluent Marin County, a nonprofit organization called Innovative Housing has brought one-parent families together with single adults and occasionally with other single-parent families to rent detached houses, generally in better areas than they could afford on their own. For sharing to have a good chance of success, Innovative Housing has found that there should be at least twice as many adults as children in the household and there should be no children younger than four years old. Most of the households that Innovative Housing has helped to form have consisted of six or seven persons.

Recently, Innovative Housing has been working on the design of new accommodations for cooperative households. As in congregate facilities for old people, the main challenge from a designer's point of view is to achieve an economical and psychologically comfortable balance between the need for privacy and the desire for contact with others. Single adults, for instance, would probably share bathrooms and a kitchen but have wash basins in their own bedrooms. Families with children would have private bathrooms and kitchenettes attached to their bedroom areas. Common areas would be placed as far away as possible from the private rooms and from the small-family subhouseholds. It seems a good idea to place the group kitchen close to the building's entrance and design the kitchen so that people can see into it before entering; this is where residents will often gather. A rear entrance could let residents avoid the social part of the house. Also, the communal TV room would need to be sealed off to prevent noise from bothering people in other rooms. Innovative Housing hopes to develop designs that may serve as prototypes, extending the concept of shared housing beyond groups such as students and the elderly, where it's already well-established.

Until now, probably the most extensive experience that for-profit builders have had with shared housing, outside the student and elderly markets, has been in constructing "mingles" units—apartments and condominiums shared by two single adults. Apartment-sharing has long been common, especially among young adults, but in the 1970s, builders and developers began to design apartments specifically to accommodate sharing. Instead of providing one large master bedroom and a smaller second bedroom that was clearly less desirable, they constructed apartments containing two bedrooms of approximately equal size, with equivalent closet space. Since the 1970s, some have produced for-sale housing embodying the same principle. Usually each bedroom is relatively large. Each may have a private patio or deck for solitude or for entertaining. One may have a private bath, while the other has access to an equally generous bath just outside the bedroom door, which guests can use as well. The rest— kitchen, dining, living area—is shared. More elaborate mingles units place each bedroom on a different floor, further reducing the potential for conflict.

The mingles unit has turned out to be virtually an all-purpose plan. It sometimes appeals to two adults who want to pool their finances to get better housing than they could otherwise afford. It appeals to some elderly people who would like companionship but who are accustomed to independence and who thus seek a home in which both residents are on a relatively equal footing. It adapts to elderly couples who sleep in separate bedrooms. It serves well for families who want a guest suite. It's also used by families who have a child old enough to want an adult-size bedroom suite; for the large number of families who have had a son or daughter move back home after a divorce or loss of a job, the second full-size bedroom suite has turned out to be decidedly attractive.

In fact, the adaptability that the dual-master-bedroom design embodies is a trait greatly needed in American housing. Today's houses are increasingly being asked to fit different needs—needs that change as time goes on. One of the growing requirements—now that computers, more sophisticated phone networks, and express mail services have made it easier to perform office functions at home—is for a place to work. Millions of people now work at home at least part-time.

Urban buildings generally lend themselves best to the increasing demand for joint working and living space. Charles A. Lagreco of the Architectural Collective in Los Angeles recently designed a six-story building on Sunset Boulevard in West Hollywood containing a mix of residential, office, and commercial space. All the units are apartmentlike in size, ranging mostly from 500 to 1,500 square feet, and they are built to switch among residential, office, and commercial uses without changing the walls or plumbing. Moreover, the units can be connected, creating either smaller or larger apartments as demand changes over time. An occupant can live in part of a unit and operate the rest as a studio or office. By making most of the units two-story, Lagreco has enhanced the ability to prevent the work area from intruding on the residential part of a unit.

There are instances in which either the budget or the owner's tastes dictate that the work area be a dominant part of the residence. The architectural firm of Moore Ruble Yudell, in Santa Monica, California, designed an inexpensive house of only 800 square feet for an artist who needed room for a small printing press; the press went on the ground floor, and a 6-by-7-foot sleeping loft was built above. But the more common practice is to enforce some kind of separation. Berkus Group Architects has often designed single-family houses with a semiautonomous guest suite—usually connected to the rest of the house, but with its own entrance and bathroom. It can then function as a workplace, master bedroom suite, or apartment—local ordinances willing. (Or perhaps even if they're not willing. It's estimated that between 1970 and 1980 as many as 2.5 million "accessory apartments" may have been established in existing single-family homes, with or without the approval of zoning and building regulations.)

Most builders and developers have not yet taken meaningful steps to deal with the question of adaptability, fraught as it is with the risk of the disapproval of local officials and the near-certainty of opposition from homeowners who are convinced that the only stable and investment-worthy neighborhood is one in which the use and occupancy of the houses are strictly delineated by law. But America has changed. The detached single-family house is no longer solely a place where children are brought up and where the only work that's done is "housework." Of all the nation's households, a mere 6 percent now consist of a working father, a mother who stays home, and two or more children. So, among architects and teachers and analysts of housing, the question is not whether American houses have to be designed differently—it's how.

A lot of ideas are being explored. Frank Dimster, a Los Angeles architect and an associate professor of architecture at the University of Southern California, designed his own family's house in the Brentwood Hills section of Los Angeles so that it could easily be subdivided. In one corner is a studio that can be closed off from the rest of the house; the studio has a sliding glass door that can function as a private entrance. Two of the house's bedrooms also have their own entrances. Near the two bedrooms is a walk-in storage room that is illuminated by a skylight. With some additional utility installation, the storage room could be converted to a kitchen and the two bedrooms turned into an apartment. Many of the nation's houses could be designed along lines like these.

Other house designs are premised on more major rearrangement. In 1984, the Minneapo-

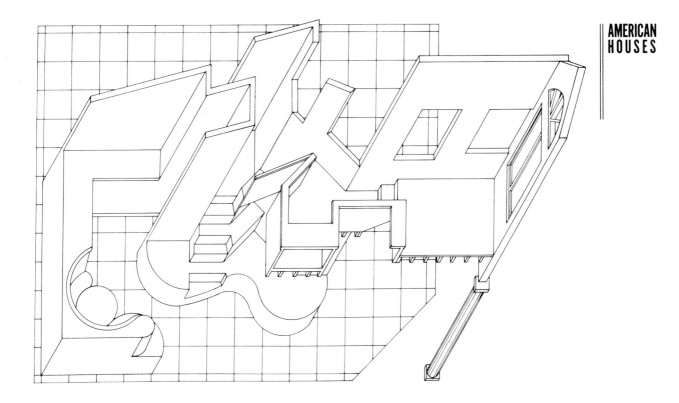

The built-in seating, the vigorous shapes, and the unimpeded flow of interior space give the King studio a dynamism and degree of comfort that more than make up for its tiny size.

lis College of Art and Design conducted a competition for a "New American House" and awarded first place to a proposal by Troy West, an architect in Wakefield, Rhode Island, and Jacqueline Leavitt, a Los Angeles urban planner. Their presentation called for a row of attached urban houses, each with an office at the front of the property and with the main portion of the house rising three stories at the property's rear. Connecting the office and the rest of the house would be a corridor kitchen alongside a private garden courtyard. The row of one-story office structures along the street would form a counterpoint to the line of attached houses at the rear. The office could be connected to a play area if a parent has to keep an eye on children, or it could function entirely independently. This proposal is not far-fetched, and one of the things that's noteworthy about it is that the design has a familiar, appealingly homelike character despite the innovations it incorporates. The houses and offices have gable roofs, and the block has a series of front yards and places for vegetable gardens.

Third-floor decks overlook the garden courts. A row of chimneys establishes a pleasant domestic rhythm above the entire complex.

How quickly changes like those proposed by West and Leavitt will be accepted into the mainstream of American home design remains to be seen, but it's safe to say that when changes come, they will not look revolutionary. In houses that adapt to changing ways of living and working, the architecture rarely sends forth trumpet blasts. Instead, trend-setting housing aims to reassure and to fit in. The small house, the mingles unit, the single-parent dwelling, the combined work-and-living quarters—all of these aspire to acceptability. In a sense, the task of the designer is first to innovate and then to encase the innovation in an atmosphere of pleasant familiarity. However the forms and features of new houses may change, the designers will find ways to connect their new creations to a long history defining how a house should look. An overlay of tradition remains, even in a time of substantial social and economic change. A house still has to look like home.

Troy West's and Jacqueline Leavitt's "New American House" proposal calls for ground-floor work areas as appendages of a row of townhouses. Garden courtyards provide close contact with nature and protected play areas for small children. The director of the competition, Minneapolis architect Harvey Sherman, has since announced plans to build houses similar to these in the Summit-University area of St. Paul.

Chapter Three

Energy
and Climate

A prefabricated solar house by Acorn Structures of Concord, Massachusetts, with collector panels on the roof. Water circulates from the panels to a 2,000-gallon storage tank in the basement.

American houses are substantially more energy-efficient than they were a dozen or more years ago. Energy, whether from oil, gas, coal, or other sources, has come to be used more sparingly. While it's impossible to say precisely how great the improvement in residential energy efficiency has been, the advances incorporated into new construction suggest that houses built today need an average of probably one-quarter less fuel for cooling than before the Arab oil embargo of 1973–1974. For space heating, the improvement has been more impressive: new houses have cut their heating requirements by one-third to one-half.

Pressure for continuing improvement fluctuates with the ups and downs of energy prices, and at this writing it's unclear whether another substantial advance will arrive soon. But the progress made since the mid-1970s seems to be permanent; it does not recede, even when energy supplies become temporarily abundant. When oil prices plummeted in 1985, for instance, the vast majority of homebuilders lost their zest for pushing energy improvements farther than they'd already gone, but few builders lowered the standards they had attained. The legacy of the Arab oil embargo endures and grows.

Immediately after the shock of the first oil disruption, a number of architects began to envision energy as the force that would generate a new architecture. A fundamental requirement of housing had drastically changed, architects reasoned, and the shape of the house, its relationship to the sun, and its response to wind and cold all demanded thorough reevaluation. For a while, it seemed possible that much of what had been customary in home design might have to be abandoned—particularly since houses built prior to 1973 had failed to use modern technology to harvest that pre-eminent, perpetual, free resource, sunshine. It was obvious that American houses would have to moderate their consumption of increasingly scarce and expensive fossil fuels, and architects around the country threw themselves into solar work. Within less than a decade, pockets of solar housing became securely established in New Mexico, Colorado, and parts of New England—places with centers of technological expertise and with either high-priced conventional forms of energy or an auspicious combination of cold winter nights and sunny winter days.

"There was a tremendous explosion of information after 1973," recalls Paul F. Pietz, an architect in Keene, New Hampshire, who became heavily involved in solar design. "Architects and architecture students grabbed onto solar as a reason for a new architecture. Here was a logic by which you could design a new house form." What ensued was a season of architectural strangeness but also of risk taking and imagination. Surely a mighty industrial civilization could master the challenge of how to capture and use energy from a source whose position in the sky every day of the year could be accurately forecast. Architects and engineers —and a lot of ordinary people who liked to tinker—set out to build houses that would attract as much sunshine as possible and convert it into usable indoor warmth.

Thus was launched a generation of "active solar" houses—"active" in that they required the operation of a mechanical system. The houses differed enormously from one another, but generally they had three things in common. First, they had some apparatus in which to gather the sun's warmth, most often panels mounted on the roof at the exact angle guaranteed to catch the maximum solar radiation. Second, inside the panels was some medium—air, water, or glycol (antifreeze) — that absorbed the sun's heat and carried it to the rest of the house. Third, since heat that was gathered on sunny days would be needed at night and on cloudy days, the houses had somewhere to store the heat — usually in a bulky tank in the basement, filled with rocks, if it was an air-based system, or with water or glycol, if it was liquid-based. Different choices entailed different handicaps. Water didn't cost much, but if it froze, it spelled disaster. Glycol, which remained liquid, could be expensive; the tank in the basement often held 2,000 gallons.

Eventually many, perhaps most, of the active-solar houses suffered major failures. All across the United States sit solar panels that are no longer connected to storage tanks or to anything else, except perhaps to someone's wounded pride. Architects grow suddenly defensive when showing slides of houses they designed in the 1970s, as if confronted by embarrassing reminders of youthful folly. Today odd roof angles intended simultaneously to capture every ray of sun and to proclaim "I am a solar house" are much less common. Awkward shapes have largely been dispensed with, and today's active-solar houses tend to assume a more conventional appearance. In Benicia, California, a subdivision of solar houses called The Village is laid out so that from cul-de-sacs and most other vantage points in the development, the roof panels are not noticeable. Active solar has turned discreet. Designers have recognized, as architect Daniel V. Scully of Peterborough, New Hampshire, expresses it, that solar energy is "just another factor to be used," not the sole criterion for shaping a house. Passions have cooled, along with many of the collector panels.

As a consequence of the widespread experimentation in the 1970s and early 1980s, active-solar mechanisms have become more reliable.

But when solar houses are built today, rarely do they strive to capture every ray of sunshine. Now a more cost-conscious attitude prevails. The active-solar houses produced by Acorn Structures, a manufacturer of housing components based in Concord, Massachusetts, exemplify the attention being devoted to economy. Rather than use 3-by-8-foot collector panels, which capture the maximum amount of solar heat per square foot but often at considerable expense, Acorn makes 4-by-20-foot panels, which are more cost-effective. The large panels are much cheaper, so the amount of heat collected per dollar spent is a far better bargain. "The point," observes Jon Slote, a solar engineer at Acorn, "is to optimize, to get the most from the least."

In some sunny parts of the country — especially California, Arizona, and Florida — and in some areas where sunshine is less abundant, such as New England, solar devices are used for the more limited purpose of helping to heat the domestic hot-water supply. These mechanisms cost less than solar space-heating systems, and they offer another advantage: whereas space heating is unlikely to be needed during the summer, hot water for washing, bathing, and kitchen uses is in demand all year long. Research is also being conducted on photovoltaic systems, which turn the sun's rays into electricity — a more versatile form of energy. The cost of photovoltaic mechanisms, although declining, still exceeds that of other solar technology, so, in the near future, photovoltaic energy is likely to remain restricted mostly to houses remote from power lines.

At least half a million houses in the United States now depend partly on solar energy, but most of these are much less complex than active-solar houses. The bulk of solar's growth has come in "passive" solar houses — dwellings

On the south face of this house, extensive expanses of glass as well as rooftop collector panels gather the sun's warmth.

by designing a series of passive-solar houses in the Chicago area in the 1930s. Libbey-Owens-Ford Glass Company extensively publicized the potential for solar after the Second World War, when the company was promoting its Thermopane dual-glazed windows. But energy remained cheap, and it wasn't until after the Arab oil embargo that passive solar began to be widely looked on as a major contributor to household heating. Then active-solar houses incorporated some passive-solar techniques to reduce the house's heating requirements, thus allowing for a less extensive array of collector panels and storage mechanisms. Gradually it became apparent that for most houses, active-solar mechanisms could be omitted and passive solar could be concentrated on.

Even in a passive-solar house, it makes sense to have some way of storing heat so that it will be available during the night. Scully placed tubes full of water near the windows of a solar house he designed in Ticonderoga, New York. The water absorbs heat when sunshine strikes the tubes, and it naturally gives off heat hours later. In Princeton, New Jersey, architect Douglas Kelbaugh pioneered the trombe wall—a heat-absorbing masonry wall—just a short distance from the house's glassy south exterior wall. In most solar architecture, these devices have since given way to less cumbersome features. The trend is toward using elements that are not just useful but attractive. Install a rock bin in the basement, and you've reduced your usable interior space without making the house look any better. If, on the other hand, you build a brick chimney wall that catches sunshine or you put down a bluestone floor over 6 inches of concrete, you have something that not only absorbs and reradiates heat but also gives your house character.

that take advantage of the sun without requiring a complicated mechanical system. Passive-solar houses position large amounts of glass on their south face so that the sun can provide immediate direct heat. Some designers make certain that there are sizable windows on the east as well, to gather sun early in the day and help the house recover quickly from the night cold. To avoid becoming too hot, the house is usually designed with little glass exposed to late afternoon and evening summertime sun on the west. North-facing windows are few or small, to reduce heat loss.

Actually, passive solar is a design technique used in various ways through much of recorded history. As early as the fifth century B.C., the Greeks began to build cities whose buildings faced due south, even on irregular terrain, and they used porticoes to keep the sun out of the houses during summer and to let it in during winter. In the United States in modern times, the architect George Fred Keck won attention

Passive solar has won acceptance in large

part because it demands no esthetic sacrifice. On the contrary, it helps to justify expenditures that otherwise would have to be made purely for appearance's sake. Handsome stonework, tiling, brick masonry, or other craftsmanship can be integrated into new houses and serve the functional rationale of reducing energy costs. Many houses today have attached greenhouses and solariums that gather heat but also provide relaxing and sunny places to sit. Passive solar does make some demands on the occupant if its energy benefits are to be fully grasped. Fans have to be turned on or doors opened to draw the warmth from the greenhouse into the rest of the home. Expanses of south-facing glass need to be covered with insulating blinds or other protection during the night if heat is to be kept from dissipating. Optimal performance is achieved only if the occupants become involved in the house's daily workings. As the saying goes, "Passive systems are for active people." But even when their energy-conserving potential isn't being pursued with much ardor, passive-solar houses are more enjoyable because of the sun, the views, and the pleasing materials.

The appearance of a passive-solar house, even more than that of an active-solar dwelling, can adopt almost whatever personality the designer and owners desire. In the Catskill Mountains in upstate New York, a house designed by Pietz exudes a Queen Anne character, accented by a long veranda, a covering of cedar shingles, and a tall, pitched roof. The major passive-solar element of this house is a sunspace that rises three stories on the south face. It has been given a nineteenth-century character. It is divided into a multitude of small panes by white muntins and mullions and culminates in a round-arched window at the peak.

By contrast, a two-story passive-solar house

The Acorn house's sunspace can distribute heat directly to the first and second stories or it can be closed off. The tile-covered concrete floor stores some warmth and emits it hours later.

in Orange, Connecticut, designed by Paul Bierman-Lytle of New Canaan, has a sleek, contemporary flavor. Its sleek, sensuous rear forms a long curve, with the breakfast room placed in the southeast corner to catch the morning sun and with the living room and study getting sun a little later in the day. On the interior of this house, which has almost no windows on the north, living areas rise two stories, permitting heat to spread naturally through the house. In winter, a fan in the peak redistributes the heat back to the lower floor and to rooms that get little direct exposure to the sun. During the summer, the fan expels heat from the house. One advantage of an open interior two or more stories high is that it generates upward air movement, helping much of

Architect Paul F. Pietz fashioned a solar house (top), *in New York's Catskill Mountains in a style suggestive of Queen Anne. He and Thomas Weller evoked Victorian styling in the house above and at left in Bloomfield, Connecticut.*

OPPOSITE
The glassy southern exposure of the Cantor house in Orange, Connecticut, by Paul Bierman-Lytle.

the heat to exit through an open skylight or other ventilation device during hot weather.

The interiors of most passive-solar houses are relatively open both vertically and horizontally, but it's also possible to arrange the house as a collection of separate rooms. On a steep hillside in Marin County, California, architects Richard Fernau and Laura Hartman of Berkeley designed a house that's laid out as a series of distinct rooms, each decorated to have an individual character. There's less of the "stack effect" to propel any excessive heat up and out, but by making the house long and thin—not much more than one room deep—the summer breezes blow in easily from the valley side in the front and continue out the back. Thinness is one attribute that most passive-solar houses have in common. The sun can penetrate only so far into a house, so a layout about one room deep encourages more even heating. Thinness is not an absolute requirement; garages, pantries, storage rooms, and other areas that don't need much heat can be placed on the north side, acting as buffers against the cold while giving the house a less elongated shape.

Solar houses rely on substantial levels of insulation, but the basic question the solar house poses is: how to pull in free energy from the outdoors? There's another way, though, to approach energy. It's to concentrate on creating strong barriers against the conditions outdoors. That a house can act and look like a barrier is illustrated by the several thousand dwellings built in the past several years with dirt mounded against their sides and on their roofs. The impact of outside cold or heat is greatly lessened when the house sits in a covering of soil. The temperature of earth changes slowly and is usually warmer than the air in winter and colder than the air in summer. If this kind of

housing was to become more popular, its proponents realized, one of the things it needed was a better image—one not burdened by the connotations of living in dim surroundings beneath the earth. The result: the term "underground house" disappeared, and in its place arrived "earth-sheltered house." The new term is not only more appealing; in some instances it's the only accurate description, since the earth may be piled against walls but not necessarily on the roof.

In Davis, California, where summertime temperatures exceed 100 degrees Fahrenheit, one section of the environmentally acclaimed Village Homes subdivision contains several earth-sheltered houses, some with three walls and a roof protected from the atmosphere, others with more of the surface exposed, accommodating more windows. Some are detached houses; others are attached side by side. In 1980, architect James Zanetto and his brother Jeff built there a 1,000-square-foot earth-sheltered house for $28,000. The south side is primarily a wall of glass. The sides and rear are covered with dirt, and on the top is 8 inches of sod, with a moistureproof barrier to keep water out. Usually an earth-sheltered house has a slight slope to its roof so that water runs off. Many earth-sheltered houses have an attractive natural cover; the Zanetto house and others at Village Homes are enveloped in the blossoms of Mediterranean and native plants.

Many earth-sheltered houses are set into hillsides or into small man-made slopes known as berms, their open side facing south. Often they have a greenhouse or large windows on the south to let in as much light as possible. But the orientation varies with the climate. In hot Southern locales, the open side of the house may face east or north. In Tucson, architect Les Wallach used another variation. He designed a 2,400-square-foot house with broad eaves and with earth berms placed 6 feet high against the heat-catching western walls, underneath the broad overhangs. The dirt was covered with rock. Because of this protection, the house needs much less air conditioning.

Earth-sheltered houses cost somewhat more than conventional dwellings, but this has not halted a rapid rise in their popularity. Bill Baker, publisher of *Earth Shelter Living,* estimates that there were 300 such houses in the United States in 1979. By 1986, Baker knew of 5,000 residential structures with an earth roof, and he believed the actual number may have been twice as high. They have been built in every state in the continental United States; the largest concentration is centered in a band from Oklahoma to Minnesota. Among other advantages, they reduce vulnerability to burglaries and tornadoes. Some companies now offer earth-sheltered houses in several standard designs — a sure sign of growing acceptance. The earth-sheltered houses proliferating the fastest are those with earth berms against the walls but no covering of dirt overhead. The reasons are several: they're easier for conventional builders to construct; they look more like a conventional house; they get a better reception from mortgage lenders; and they're not as costly, since the roof doesn't have to be engineered for such a heavy load.

What about the kinds of houses that most Americans live in? In these, the degree of attention to energy varies greatly. Some major builders have adopted passive-solar designs and found an enthusiastic market for them, but progress in this direction differs widely from one region to another. On the whole, solar housing remains the province of individuals and of small companies that take pains with each house they construct. Big builders, especially those operating in many different metropolitan areas, have basically ignored solar considerations.

The obliviousness to solar reveals itself most blatantly in the placement of windows. In subdivisions in Phoenix — one of the busiest home-building markets of the 1980s — it's common to see brand-new houses containing large windows that face south or west, unsheltered from the summertime sun — this in a city where temperatures reach a broiling 110 degrees Fahrenheit under a bright, cloudless sky. Windows like these are uncomfortable to sit next to even in the spring and fall, and obviously they aggravate the need for air conditioning.

Drive through a new subdivision — not only in Phoenix, but in most areas of the country — and frequently you'll find a series of differing exteriors, intended to give some visual variety to houses with nearly identical floor plans. One house will have a gable roof that exposes windows to the scalding summertime sun, while the house next door will have a hip roof providing at least partial protection. In a situation like this, a discerning homebuyer will look carefully at where the windows are placed, how much protection they'll get from overhangs or other devices during hot months, and how much sun they're likely to catch during cold months — and then will take these factors into account when deciding which house to buy. Builders have continued to settle on window sizes according to whether the windows face the street or the backyard, without considering whether the windows face north, south, east, or west — with the result that an unconscionably large number of houses in cold states have their biggest windows facing north and many houses in hot climates have large, unshaded windows facing south or west. Houses on one side of the street will be more comfortable and more

Because of its long, thin shape, the Maoli house in Marin County, California, by Richard Fernau and Laura Hartman, is cooled in the summer by hillside breezes that pass easily through its rooms. The east elevation shown here is segmented into a series of projecting rooms that have windows on their southern exposure to capture sun when needed.

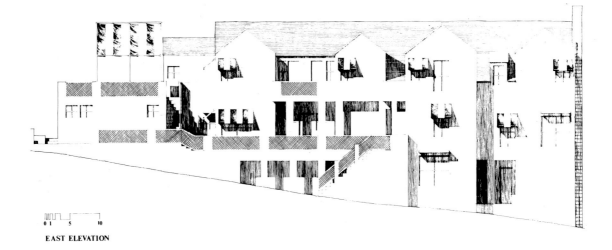

0 1   5   10

EAST ELEVATION

OPPOSITE
Houses using a covering of earth as relief from the 100-degree-plus heat in Davis, California (bottom), *and from freezing winter temperatures in Colorado* (top). *The Colorado house is entered through a stone arch topped by soil.*

energy-efficient than the houses on the other; the attentive buyer will choose accordingly. Another simple matter that can make an impact on energy consumption is the location of a garage or carport. Many builders are willing to flip a floor plan and build the garage or carport on the end where it will work best with the climate. In much of the nation, a garage on the north or west wall can blunt the winter winds. A garage on the south or west can block unwanted heat from the summer sun. Buyers should ask builders what's being done to design and construct the house so that, from the standpoint of energy and comfort, it works well on its site. If the answers aren't satisfactory, find another builder.

Passive solar can easily be incorporated into detached houses if the builder is willing to modify the design to fit the site. Attached housing poses more obstacles. As density increases, the requirements of security, privacy, and circulation patterns collide more sharply with energy concerns. Ralph Knowles, a solar architecture authority at the University of Southern California, has done research demonstrating that it's feasible to develop passive-solar housing at up to 40 units an acre, but, in practice, even the architects and builders who are interested in passive solar rarely pursue it in complexes of more than 20 units an acre. A prospective buyer or tenant, however, can check on which units have glass in advantageous locations and can select a unit partly on that basis. Often there are sizable differences in solar access within a single development.

━━━━

The key fact about the housing industry's response to energy is that most builders don't want to be bothered to try to design each house individually to respond to the energy conditions of its site. Builders have achieved great improvements in energy performance, but the progress has little to do with site planning and window placement. The advances lie instead in the realm of construction—how much insulation is installed, how walls are built to block drafts, what kinds of windows are chosen. The progress can be measured in R-values— measures of heat flow in which the higher the number, the better the house's ability to master its energy situation. Ceilings are the largest single source of energy loss in houses. In 1973, the average detached house had ceilings with an R-value of 13; by 1984, the average had doubled, to 26. The R-value of side walls, not counting their sheathing, rose from about 9 in 1973 to more than 12 in 1984. The sheathing itself improved markedly. Over studwalls packed with insulating batts, some builders place an insulating rigid-foam sheathing that's much more effective than its predecessor, plywood, at boosting the wall's ability to resist the passage of heat. Hidden under many a home's veneer of brick, clapboard, or other siding is a tough plastic membrane, DuPont's Tyvek, designed to reduce air infiltration, especially infiltration caused by wind.

The use of insulating glass or storm windows has more than doubled since 1973, and some of the insulating glass introduced in the past few years possesses extraordinary capabilities. Early in the 1980s, U.S. manufacturers such as the 3M Company in Minnesota and Southwall Technologies in Palo Alto, California, began producing film that is placed between panes of insulating glass, creating an additional dead-air pocket to reduce the transmission of heat between indoors and out. Southwall developed a film called Heat Mirror that actually *reflects* warmth. A thin layer of metal oxide lets sunlight and near-infrared radiation pass through, but it bounces back the radiant energy generated by a furnace or given off by objects within a house. In contrast to a single-glazed window's R-value of 1, dual-pane glass equipped with Heat Mirror registers an impressive 4.3. Other manufacturers put a similar coating directly on one of the panes of glass. Windows with these coated films or coated glass are called "low-emissivity" or "low-E" windows, since they emit lower amounts of radiant energy. Low-E coatings are meant to be invisible, but under certain light conditions, most of them have a faint blue or gray cast. Beyond saving on fuel bills, low-E windows make a substantial difference in comfort. The interior surface of the glass stays closer to room temperature, so in a house in a cold climate, people can sit next to a window without their body heat being drawn to the glass. Recent variations on low-E glass cater to the needs of hot climates, blocking a higher proportion of solar heat while admitting ample light, or combining low-E with tinted glass. So it's possible to offset some of the effect of having windows facing the hot summer sun.

Homebuilding practices are growing steadily more stringent. In the North, builders have moved toward the use of exterior doors containing a core of insulation that prevents heat from going through easily. Some use magnetic weather stripping along the door edges to help stop air leaks. Many builders are sealing joints more thoroughly, and some are insulating foundation walls on either the outside or the inside.

Mechanical equipment is also improving. The use of heat pumps, which in moderate climates are more economical to operate than conventional forced-air electrical furnaces, has more than doubled since 1973. Central air-conditioning systems have been installed in about two-thirds of new American houses, but some of the equipment is designed to achieve higher efficiency than before, and alternatives

to heavy use of air conditioning are gaining acceptance. Ceiling fans have come back in fashion, creating breezes that make hot weather more tolerable and taking heat from the ceiling in winter and redirecting it downward. In the South, whole-house fans, installed in the attic, have experienced a revival. When turned on at night, they pull in cool outside air and expel hot air through the top of the house. In the morning, the fan can be turned off, the windows shut, and the house kept reasonably cool without air conditioning until later in the day.

Many states have adopted building codes mandating improved energy performance. Some set specific standards for R-values in walls or ceilings, for example. Other codes, such as Florida's, establish an overall performance standard, giving builders and designers flexibility on how to achieve it. The amount of insulation in the ceiling, for instance, can be balanced against the efficiency rating of the air-conditioning equipment. California's energy code permits variation according to the climate of different geographical areas. In addition, institutions that finance mortgages have given builders incentives to upgrade energy efficiency by liberalizing some of the mortgage underwriting standards when it can be shown that the house is likely to incur lower utility costs. The major force behind the advances in energy conservation now, though, is not governments or institutions—it's popular demand for more comfortable, less wasteful houses.

A substantial number of builders, scattered mostly through the North, have gone far beyond any regulatory requirements and erected what are called "superinsulated" houses—the most efficient houses yet built in the United States. These are houses with plenty of insulation, as the term implies, but what's crucial is that the 121

*Behind the vertical glass of Kelbaugh & Lee Architects'
Mills-Wright residence in Chatham, New Jersey, a black-
surfaced concrete block trombe wall extends from below
ground level into the second story, radiating warmth and
supporting the second floor. Beneath the sloping glass is
the whirlpool room. Metal fins attached to copper pipes
just below the sloping glass catch the sun and help to
heat the house's water supply.*

123

insulation is installed exceedingly carefully as part of a comprehensive effort to make the houses snug and nearly airtight. Some super-insulated houses employ passive-solar designs with many windows on the south and few on the north, but not all do.

Indeed, the energy that builders of super-insulated houses often talk about capturing is the heat given off by the occupants and their appliances. A family of 4 can generate 2,000 British thermal units an hour in body heat. The appliances in a typical kitchen may generate an average of 1,200 BTUs an hour. Lights and miscellaneous electrical sources may give off another 1,000 BTUs or more, for a total "free" heat in excess of 4,200 BTUs an hour. In the typical house, this heat is of no importance at all; the average house built since 1950 leaks so badly through and around its windows, doors, fans, light fixtures, partitions, foundation joints, electrical boxes, and other building components that, in a single hour, 60–70 percent of the house's air is replaced—nearly all of it unintentionally—by incoming unconditioned air. Newly built houses are better, on average replacing probably half their air in an hour. Still, in winters like those in upstate New York, even a relatively small detached house built to current standards of construction can, through air infiltration and other means of heat loss, surrender 20,000 BTUs an hour.

But what if the loss of heat were reduced so dramatically that the warmth generated inside the house stayed put? Presumably, the utility bills could be much smaller, or so it seemed to a number of individuals and organizations—including the U.S. Department of Housing and Urban Development and the Saskatchewan Research Council—that in the 1970s got involved in constructing a series of exceptionally tightly built houses in Arkansas, Illinois, Massachu-

setts, and Saskatchewan. Thirty-five Arkansas houses with a number of features unusual at the time, such as R-19 fiberglass insulation in walls 6 inches thick, achieved average annual heating and cooling costs of only about $130 in 1974–1975.

The most astounding example of what could be done was the Saskatchewan Conservation House, built in Saskatoon by a Canadian team in 1977. It had walls a foot thick with R-44 insulation and a ceiling with insulation exceeding R-60. So airtight was this house that the annual heating cost would be $35 (Canadian) at 1978 prices. The Saskatchewan house was also extremely ugly, with a nearly two-story mansard roof awkwardly pressing down toward a line of three drab picture windows on the first floor. But its ungainly esthetics didn't matter. Builders and designers realized that its principles could be incorporated into houses that could take on whatever appearance the owner wanted. The Saskatchewan house proved that even in a bitterly cold climate, it was possible to design and build a comfortable house that would function with the warmth generated by occupants, appliances, and lights, supplemented in some cases by a minimal amount of additional heat.

Since 1980, superinsulated houses have proliferated throughout the northern United States. In the farm country south of Rochester, New York, where winters are severe (as measured by heating degree-days that total more than 7,000 a year) and where the winter wind *averages* 12 miles an hour, R. John Magar and his company, Magar Homes, began building super-insulated houses in 1982, drawing on the Saskatchewan experience. For Carl and Helen Chichester and their 2 children, he built a 1,276-square-foot, 3-bedroom house so meticulously insulated and sealed that it needed no furnace. Magar supplied a quartz space heater in case the house didn't perform as expected, but by the end of the first winter the family had used a total of 64 cents' worth of electricity to operate it, and during the second winter they didn't use the heater at all. "I don't think I've ever put a sweater on," Helen Chichester said. "In the morning when I get up, I turn on a kitchen light, and within 15 minutes it's warm."

The house, which has as many windows as an ordinary house and is conventional in design except for its energy-conserving features, cost about $5,000–$6,000 more than if it had been built by routine methods. A key difference in construction is the walls, which in the Magar-built house are 14 inches thick and composed of 3 layers. On the inside is a 2-by-4 framework, on the exterior is a second 2-by-4 framework, and in between is a 7-inch space. All three layers are packed with cellulose fiber, giving the walls an extraordinary R-60 insulation value and making it impossible for the wooden wall studs to transfer heat from the interior to the outside. Ceilings have the same R-60 rating.

Thick though the insulation is, it does not fully explain why the house functions so well in the cold. What matters just as much is that Magar diligently eliminated leaks. He used 100 tubes of silicone sealant to plug every tiny opening that could have let cold air seep in. He installed dual-glazed windows and then covered them with one set of storm windows on the outside and a second set on the inside. He mounted the electrical outlets on the surfaces of the walls, rather than puncturing the walls and enabling heat to escape. He installed a wood foundation because it does not conduct heat as easily as one of concrete. The basement floor is concrete, but underneath is a plastic sheet that prevents moisture transmission. In the summer,

when the warmth being generated indoors isn't wanted, the Chichesters simply open the windows and the house becomes nearly as well ventilated as an ordinary house. Superinsulation is best suited to winter needs—keeping "free" warmth in and cold air out—but in a climate where the objective is to prevent the hot outdoor atmosphere from getting in, super-insulation offers an extremely effective barrier against incoming heat.

Methods of superinsulation vary from one builder to another, but in every case the effectiveness of the insulation depends on attention to detail; it is a system that, like plumbing, doesn't allow for leaks. A large builder unable to train and motivate an extensive number of work crews may find superinsulation too demanding. And some builders, such as Pittsburgh-based Ryan Homes, contend that for first-time home-buyers with moderate incomes, the extra cost of superinsulation drives the price of the house too high. Superinsulated houses are mostly the product of small builders who supervise their workers closely and who may do some of the labor themselves. The scrupulous care on which superinsulation depends can also be obtained under factory conditions. Buffalo Homes, in Butte, Montana, has manufactured high-quality three-bedroom modular ranch houses with ratings of R-38 in the walls and R-60 in the ceilings. The electric heating bill for one such house for a full year totaled $29.98—this in a harsh Montana climate calculated to exceed 8,000 heating degree-days a year. (In comparison, there are 4,848 degree-days in an average heating season in New York City and 3,095 in Atlanta.) Superinsulation is one of the most effective responses yet to the nation's long-term energy problems. Authorities such as J. D. Ned Nisson, coauthor with Gautam Dutt of *The Superinsulated Home Book,* expect that super-

Plastic tubes filled with water capture and later give off some of the sun's warmth in a house in Ticonderoga, New York, by Daniel V. Scully.

A jazzy Postmodern tower expels excess heat from a Connecticut house designed by Centerbrook's William H. Grover.

insulation will eventually win a substantial following in the South because of rapidly rising electricity costs for air conditioning in parts of that region.

There's a romantic-traditional alternative to an approach like this. In recent years, a number of architects have been searching for ways to build that are in harmony with nature and enriched by a sense of the past. In the years before air conditioning, houses across much of the South were built with a wide central passageway that sat under the same roof as the house's enclosed rooms but was open at both ends to let breezes blow through. Some of these "dog-trot" houses, as they were unceremoniously called, were elevated above ground level, and they rose to a central belvedere or ventilating cupola, allowing the rising hot air to exit naturally through the top of the house. This folk tradition largely disappeared by the late 1940s, but now it has captured some designers' imaginations. In Tampa in the late 1970s, for instance, Rowe Holmes Barnett Architects revived and modernized the form of the dog-trot house for a new home. Where the old houses had their dog-trot or breezeway, the Tampa house positions its kitchen and dining and living areas, all rela-

Heat-collecting sunspace of a house at Brookhaven National Laboratory, Long Island, New York.

Adobe-style passive solar in La Vereda Compound in Santa Fe, New Mexico, designed and built by Wayne and Susan Nichols's Communico Inc.

tively open and with sliding screen doors on each end to let the air come through. On two sides of this open central area are the bedrooms. Just as the old dog-trot houses had vents in the floor and ceiling to assist air circulation, the 2,000-square-foot Tampa house has vents in the bedroom ceilings that open into an attic and from there into the belvedere, from which hot air escapes through clerestory windows.

The occupants of the Tampa house report that it works well; rarely do they use mechanical air conditioning. During the winter, the vents and openings can be closed to keep the heat inside (though certainly not as thoroughly as in a superinsulated house). Since 1979, duplicates of this house have been built across the South from Florida and South Carolina to Texas, using plans that the owners allowed to be sold. We cannot say that its handling of climate has been the reason for this dog-trot design's far-ranging popularity; apparently the critical factor is that the house is raised a full story above the ground. Most of the builders were looking for attractive ways to erect houses in coastal areas vulnerable to flooding. Nonetheless, the dog-trot house does offer a generally workable way of dealing with climate and energy considerations. **127**

In the architectural community's now-widespread reconsideration of the merits of historical architecture, the features of folk or "vernacular" design are getting a close and increasingly cordial inspection. Folk architecture, over generations, developed features that embodied a certain commonsense wisdom, features that responded to the climate and made the seasons more enjoyable. On a 450-acre ranch in the Texas hill country, Austin architect Lawrence W. Speck designed a 2,200-square-foot house that uses some elements of old rural Texas dwellings. The house, built with the metal roof and limestone walls common in nineteenth-century hill-country houses, has extensive porches, some facing south, others north, for use at different times of day and in different seasons. In fact, the porches cover more space than the house's interior does. Some of them adjoin bedrooms so that beds can be moved outside, recalling the "sleeping porches" that were common decades ago.

It's interesting to juxtapose these examples of the vernacular revival against superinsulated houses because they suggest two opposing attitudes about energy, about climate, even about the house's place on the land. Vernacular houses accommodate themselves to the climate, using architectural features such as porches, breezeways, and belvederes to provide a measure of comfort for their occupants. The houses' shapes and placement acknowledge the importance of nature and mitigate disagreeable aspects of the climate. It's not surprising that, amid the environmental consciousness of the past two decades, many thoughtful people have decided to learn from traditional kinds of houses that are at ease with the climate and with their surroundings in general. More such houses are likely to be constructed in the next few years,

working out a low-tech accommodation between climate and comfort.

And yet any realistic examination of American houses underscores the fact that vernacular approaches are not going to be the dominant American way of dealing with energy. They ameliorate the discomfort of the climate but never overcome it entirely. The more telling vision of where the United States is headed is the superinsulated house. Superinsulation is a building method that puts its faith in applied technology, that uses fiberglass and silicone, polyethylene, and other synthetic materials to defy the constraints of nature. Superinsulated houses can stand wherever their owners choose to put them—a critical advantage to the many Americans who are moving to places like Arizona and are currently relying on conventional construction methods and vast volumes of air conditioning to make their houses habitable in the long, hot seasons of the year. People today are less willing to tolerate uncomfortable cold or heat than were the occupants of vernacular houses years ago. And while most builders are unlikely to go quite so far as Magar or the Saskatchewan team in reducing energy needs, more of them can be expected to follow those examples at least partway.

The primary drawback of the superinsulated house, aside from its higher initial investment, is that it requires a forced ventilation system. The houses built by Magar, for instance, have a natural air-change rate in the winter of only 4 percent an hour, which isn't enough to get rid of contaminants in indoor air. Houses collect gases and chemical substances from a large number of sources, including carbon monoxide from gas stoves, radioactive radon gas from soil and rock in some regions, and formaldehyde from particle board, wallpaper, other building products, and many household furnishings. In a conventional leaky house, air infiltration dilutes and eventually expels such substances, although not in a systematic way; pollutants may accumulate in the bathroom, bedrooms, and basement even while the air in the living room changes.

Regardless of whether ordinary houses need mechanical ventilation (they do, according to some superinsulation advocates), there is no question that such systems are a necessity in superinsulated houses. Specialists in superinsulation recommend installing a ventilation system that replaces 30–40 percent of the house's air each hour. The Chichester house, for example, was outfitted with an air exchanger that continuously expels stale air and recaptures more than 80 percent of the outgoing air's heat, transferring the warmth to the incoming fresh air. In the South, where superinsulation is used mostly to keep the interior cool, the technique is at a comparative disadvantage in that the heat generated by bodies, appliances, and lights was of no use. Newer kinds of ventilators, however, can take the heat that's being expelled from the house and transfer it into the domestic hot-water supply, eliminating the homeowner's hot-water heating bills.

The number of intensively superinsulated houses being built can be expected to fluctuate from year to year, but the basic objective—a well-insulated house far more tightly sealed than the houses of the past—appears destined to become more widely shared. Even when energy prices occasionally drop, people do not revert to inefficient pre-1973 building practices. Some builders may relax slightly, but, in general, the improvements in energy conservation are absorbed into standard practice. Most new construction settles on an energy-performance plateau, and when prices resume their rise again, houses make a further advance.

It has turned out that the most conspicuous advocates of energy efficiency in the mid-1970s—those who built active-solar houses—were mistaken in thinking that American houses would come to depend on elaborate solar mechanisms and that the shapes and siting of houses would change. They've been proven right, though, about the overall direction of house construction—toward the use of an increasingly sophisticated technology to master the energy situation and attain the comfort that people expect. Houses are evolving into complex systems—structures capable of creating a separate world indoors, far removed from the conditions outside. They may not look much different, but they're now freer than they've ever been from the constraints of climate.

ABOVE

Platt house in Guilford, Connecticut—by Kent Bloomer, David Conger, and Paul Bierman-Lytle—uses a tile-covered concrete slab floor and a massive Russian fireplace to absorb and gradually release heat.

RIGHT

The Bloom house in Guilford has a solar atrium from which heat can be blown into a rock bed beneath the living room, for retrieval later. Sun coming through lower slopes of glass can directly warm the kitchen and living room on ground floor. At night or in hot weather, insulating panels slide into place on horizontal rafters.

OPPOSITE TOP

Passive solar townhouses in La Vereda Compound sit within Santa Fe's registered historic district; thus their style.

OPPOSITE BOTTOM

Windows on a sculpted house in Guilford, Connecticut, by Steven Conger, David Conger, and Paul Bierman-Lytle. By contrast, the northern exposure is covered almost entirely in wood.

Chapter Four

Construction and Craftsmanship

The dramatic introduction of sunlight from above as well as from sloping window-walls emphasizes the varying tone of the clear Western red cedar in a Southampton, New York, house by architect Norman Jaffe.
OVERLEAF
Carpenters placing a barge rafter — hasu in Japanese — for the roof of a house by Len Brackett in Tiburon, California.

Are American homes well built? The very question summons up longstanding doubts about the nation's housing—doubts that persist despite the abundance of ways in which problems, once they are identified, can be corrected. These misgivings concern two fundamentally different kinds of issues. One is the house's physical performance—does it keep water out, is the electrical system reliable, do edges, surfaces, and corners remain true? The basic concern here is the sturdiness and functional adequacy of the materials and the method of construction. The second line of inquiry focuses on more esthetic and subjective matters—are the windows well proportioned, the walls appropriately finished, the ceilings pleasing to the eye?

Sturdiness or functional adequacy is clearly the more crucial concern. No matter how handsome a house may look, it won't last if it cannot satisfy the physical demands placed on it. This is the reality that building codes address. Yet the importance of craftsmanship, of finishes, of pleasingly individual touches, ought not to be underestimated. A house is an intimate environment—one that, at its best, can carry on cultural traditions and nourish and elevate daily life. Neither physical adequacy nor esthetic quality is really expendable.

The low point for sturdiness of construction in the twentieth century was probably the decade immediately following the Second World War. Suddenly homes were being built in massive numbers. In place of the trickle of residential construction during the 1930s and the restricted homebuilding of the war years, a torrent of civilian construction—encouraged by government-insured mortgages—flooded developing suburbs in the late 1940s and 1950s. In the hurry to house the beginning of America's baby boom, some of the earlier pride of workmanship disappeared, and there were few warranties or consumer protection agencies to hold builders accountable for their failings. During this period, newer materials, including plywood and plasterboard, and more modern methods, such as prefabrication, increasingly made their way into homebuilding. Many problems ensued. Doors warped, walls buckled, basements leaked. Sometimes even the wiring didn't work. This was the inauspicious start of a widespread shift to more efficient ways of erecting houses.

Since this initial burst of postwar construction, much of the homebuilding industry has continued to move gradually away from traditional materials and old construction methods. How many builders use brick the way it was employed in the old row houses of Brooklyn, Baltimore, and Philadelphia—as solid, load-bearing walls two or three bricks thick? Certainly the majority do not. Brick is now usually treated as a veneer, attached to a structural framework made up of wooden studs, And the kind of wood used by homebuilders today is, in some respects, inferior to what was available a century ago. Forest stands that had been growing for more than 200 years, offering long, straight timber with few knots, were felled long ago, and their replacements are often smaller, fast-grown trees yielding less clear wood. As Donald Baerman, an adjunct professor of architecture at Yale University, observed, "We took the best first." The dimensions of today's wooden components have decreased, too. Those acquainted with carpentry are aware that the two-by-four, measured dry, is actually 1½ by 3½ inches.

Such changes can be seen as evidence of a general decline in construction quality, but what often escapes notice is a countering trend—the dissemination of more systematic knowledge about materials and building techniques. Homeowners who look with dismay at the shrunken lumber going into today's houses are to some extent being misled by their own eyes; they may not realize that lumber with bigger dimensions went into older houses in part because there was uncertainty about wood and about houses. Builders didn't know precisely how large the house's structural load would be, and they didn't know how much weight and force the house's wooden structural elements could actually carry. They compensated for their limited knowledge by putting in large members "just in case," adding an implicit safety factor.

Today, by contrast, structural loads are much better understood, and there are readily available means of determining lumber's moisture content and strength. Lumber undergoes "stress grading" and is labeled to reflect the results. Years of testing have enabled lumber to emerge as something that construction specialists like to call "an engineered material" with a known strength. A builder today who wants to span a certain distance, with wood that will carry an anticipated defined load, can turn to a species-specific chart and find, for instance, that two-by-fours of kiln-dried Southern pine #2, placed every 2 feet, will safely span 14 feet and carry a live load of 40 pounds per square foot. The more scientific basis of today's construction provides builders with a reliable indication of the structural quality of the materials, and it allows a builder to provide sufficient strength without wasting resources.

The reliability of today's houses also stems from the use of components made under controlled conditions. Since the early 1950s, housing has undergone a creeping industrialization as building components have increasingly been produced by factories, subject to quality-assurance procedures. In 1952, a connector plate was invented that made it feasible to construct a roof truss. No longer did the builder need to have carpenters hammer individual roof rafters and ceiling joists together at every homesite. Today the factory-made roof truss—a triangular framework of two-by-fours with metal plates—is used in approximately 95 percent of new site-built houses. In 1970, the floor truss was invented. Today it is used in probably 80 percent of America's site-built houses. Prehung doors and preassembled stairs—less subject to warping and deficient construction—have become commonplace. Increasingly builders are adopting "panelized" construction, in which an entire wall—complete with windows, doors, wiring, exterior siding, and interior finishes—is produced in a factory and quickly erected at the building site.

Many new materials have come into use. Silicone sealants, rigid-foam insulation, plastic membranes that control moisture transmission and air infiltration, window films that hold radiant heat inside the house or keep it outside—these and other substances have helped to bring about a marked improvement in weatherproofing and energy efficiency since the early 1970s. Heating devices such as electrical heat pumps have been refined. Wiring and electrical systems have been upgraded.

The next generation of advances is likely to concentrate on components that contain synthetic materials and that can fulfill more than one function at the same time—wall materials, for instance, that provide both structural strength and insulating value. Arco Building Products in Philadelphia recently introduced its "Wallframe Building System," which consists of 4-by-8-foot wall panels made mostly of expanded polystyrene, the material used for years as white foam coffee cups. The panels come

Lightweight Wallframe building panels arriving at a homesite.

Four-by-eight-foot panels assembled into an entire wall.

either 3½ inches thick, producing an R-value of 15, or 5½ inches thick, delivering an R-value of 23. They eliminate wall studs, which allow heat and cold to pass through walls built with conventional construction methods. And the company claims that no vapor barrier has to be installed in the wall cavity, since moisture has hardly any effect on polystyrene. Galvanized steel strips are molded into the interior and exterior sides of the panels, supporting the weight that would ordinarily be carried by wooden studs. Gypsumboard on the interior and siding on the exterior can be nailed directly onto the steel straps. How quickly the Wallframe innovation will be adopted remains to be seen, but a number of companies are working on advances of this sort.

Construction problems still arise, but sporadically, affecting only a minority of new houses. They arise in part because more scientific standards have not eliminated all the problems with materials. Most species of wood, for instance, will warp if they're sold and stored without proper precautions. Consequently, even though there are grading standards, some unfit lumber still arrives at the homesite. A conscientious builder discards defective lumber or sends it back, but a lax builder may use it anyway and cause potential problems for the occupants. For the things that can go wrong in homebuilding, industrialization is by no means a cure-all. There are builders and developers who extensively regrade the land and, instead of giving the earth time to settle, promptly put houses on it—houses that soon begin to shift. The occupants start to find that windows won't go up and down smoothly, and they have no idea that the reason is the unstable ground. In more extreme cases, the house may settle so much that foundation walls crack and let water inside.

If you had to pick a city where construction shortcuts are especially rampant, Houston would be a leading contender. It's ironic that Houston, which prides itself as a citadel of free enterprise, is the American city whose building practices most call to mind the notorious sloppiness of construction in the Soviet Union. Drive through subdivisions on Houston's outskirts and you can see roofers nailing asphalt-

Installed panels, which eliminate separate framing, insulation, and sheathing.

The finished house is visually indistinguishable from conventional construction.

composition shingles directly onto plywood decking without first installing building paper — an inexpensive black asphaltic and felt paper designed to shed any water that gets under the shingles. Some of Houston's roofers also don't bother to install metal channels in the "valleys" where two sloping roofs intersect. Instead, they overlap the shingles across the V-shaped juncture, virtually guaranteeing that well before the shingles on the main slopes of roof have reached the end of their expected 20-year life span, the valley will have been so eroded by rainstorms that repairs will be needed.

Even when the roofing is installed correctly, there may be water problems at ground level. In some Houston subdivisions, downspouts empty into rubber tubes that carry the rain water just a few feet from the house and then spill the contents onto the flat surface of the land — not into a storm sewer, a drainage ditch, or anything else capable of handling major rainstorms. The inadequate drainage system virtually invites water to seep into the houses. Some "affordable" houses have been built with plastic doorknobs on interior doors and with window sills consisting of nothing more than wallpaper pasted onto gypsumboard. Potentially troublesome construction practices abound in other parts of Texas, too. Go into builders' model homes in midwinter and you may see water trickling from every spigot. The spigots have been left open because the plumbing system is inadequately protected against freezing, and the only way the builder prevents burst pipes is by keeping the water in motion. Many Texas houses have been built with insulation above the ceiling and with pipes placed above the insulation; consequently, during colder-than-normal winters, the water in some of the pipes turns to ice, breaks the pipes, soaks the insulation, and brings the ceiling crashing down.

Most American houses, fortunately, are built to a higher standard. Across the United States, the emphasis on quality in construction is especially pronounced in regions with cold climates. Warranty programs, consumer protection agencies, underwriting standards, and government regulations have all served to limit the extent of shoddy construction.

The strength of the variations between home-building in one area and in another can be surprising. This is especially true of craftsmanship and attention to esthetics. A booming local economy—presumably creating a demand even for poorly-built houses—cannot by itself explain the variations. Houston and Atlanta have both ranked among the four busiest homebuilding areas in the nation through much of the 1980s, and yet the contrast between the two cities is enormous. In Houston, craftsmanship is often mediocre; craftsmanship in Atlanta is frequently impressive. Many Northern builders relocating to Atlanta have felt compelled to raise their standards because using materials well and consistently is a major concern there.

Some Atlanta houses display a brick veneer on only the façade, like millions of houses elsewhere in the United States, but in quite a number, brick encases the entire house, giving it an appearance of solidity. Masons make knowledgeable use of a greater variety of mortar joints, and they tend more often to limit the bricks on any one house to a narrow range of color, giving the house a dignity all too often lacking in houses in other regions, where the mixing of contrasting light and dark tones produces a circuslike effect. Some expensive homes use brick on the visible portions of foundation walls as well, further dressing up the house.

In Atlanta, roofs are often built at a steeper pitch, giving the house greater presence, even though the higher roof costs more. Where roofs in many parts of the country rise 4 feet in height for every 12 feet of horizontal distance, houses in Atlanta may have a roof pitch of 5 or 6 in 12. Overhangs, which make a house look more substantial and also add to the construction cost, are deeper.

In Atlanta houses in upper price ranges, the interior woodwork can be magnificent. Some houses constructed by Chathambilt Homes, a leading builder in Atlanta's affluent northern suburbs, have tall foyers distinguished by winding staircases whose handrails are made by laboriously bowing and fitting together seven long, thin strips of wood to form a single continuous curve. Many of these houses have wide fluted casings on doors and 3-inch crown moldings in places such as the master bedroom. The best of them boast family rooms or "great rooms" with walls outfitted from floor to ceiling in glowing birch, oak, or hickory—4-by-8-foot sheets of it, with 6-inch-wide trim boards covering the seams and with moldings along the trim boards' edges to give the woodwork a refined detailing. The builders call this "judges' paneling," a term intended to give the woodwork some extra allure, but such selling-through-semantics is superfluous; the woodwork surpasses the quality of many halls of justice.

It's tempting to regard features like these simply as expressions of general upper-income taste—of wealth independent of geography or local history—but the fact is that from one metropolitan area to another, there remain strong differences in the degree of craftsmanship even within segments of homebuilding oriented toward the same class or income group. You can find beautifully paneled doors, parquet floors, and leaded-glass cabinets in expensive houses in the Los Angeles area, for instance, but usually the houses as a whole aren't as consistently well crafted as those that appeal to the same class of homebuyers in Atlanta. In Los Angeles, fine materials and careful workmanship embellish the main exterior wall, the double-height foyer, and a few other prominent areas, but as with a Hollywood set, once you go backstage you find that the sumptuous effects are a front—unlike the situation in Atlanta,

Silhouettes in stucco along a townhouse patio garden at The Cottonwoods of Anozira, in Tempe, Arizona.

where quality goes deeper than the façade. Some regions have a clearer understanding that craftsmanship is not the same as conspicuous consumption.

The industrialization that's generally brought more efficiency and reliability to homebuilding has had a mostly detrimental effect on esthetics. Builders have entered into a competition to keep their labor and materials costs down, but just as important, they've gotten into a race against time, and craftsmanship has fared badly as a result of all of this. Plastering, which invited the occupants of even modest middle-class houses to look up and admire delicate patterning on ceilings, could not compete against gypsumboard. Builders didn't want to wait while

the plasterer applied three successive coats, allowing time for each to dry. The process was speeded by panels of gypsumboard (also called "drywall" or referred to by the trade name "Sheetrock"). It's true that today's drywall is a better product than the plasterboard of the 1940s; its joints, properly taped, are smoother and sturdier. It is also less troublesome to repair than plaster that has started to crumble. It has a smoothness, too, that complements a minimalist esthetic. But in most cases, there's nothing all that wonderful about the fact that the walls or ceilings possess smoothness; so does a

OVERLEAF
*The tile friezes add distinction to the exterior of
Cuernavaca Villas in Tucson, Arizona.*

141

cardboard box. And many of the gypsumboard ceilings are machine-sprayed with a mix of plaster and paint. The cottage-cheese texture—intended to conceal possible imperfections, especially in the long slopes of vaulted ceilings—has the look of having been fashioned by a machine, not by graceful sweeps of the human hand.

In speeding and simplifying construction, builders have also eliminated many of the moldings that once were commonplace. There may be no moldings at the juncture of wall and ceiling and no casings around doorways. Baseboards are often thin and tiny, barely enough to anchor a doorstop. Factory-made components often economize severely on appearance; prehung windows, for instance, generally come with narrow casings that give the window a meager look. However, in certain areas, such as Washington, D.C., some tract homebuilders in the past few years have begun a heartening trend toward enlarging the window casings and base moldings and reintroducing cornice moldings. And one of the skills of large residential architectural firms like Berkus Group Architects and Fisher-Friedman Associates lies in detailing house exteriors so that they project a bolder, more generous personality. A seemingly minor item like the size of the window casings can make a big difference in the house's visual character.

Fisher-Friedman once conducted a survey of homebuyers' preferences and discovered a strong desire for better doors. Builders are well aware of the importance of the front door; carved and paneled doors show up on many upper-income homes. But inside the house are often hollow-core or other lightweight doors, which, like thin moldings, give a sense of architectural impoverishment. The growing interest in old houses over the past two decades has

been spurred in part by just such things as doors that feel right—objects that have weight and pleasing detail. The builders of new homes should take notice.

———

Nowhere is the issue of architectural reduction for the sake of economy more evident—and more difficult to resolve—than in America's most industrialized form of housing, the mobile home. In recent years, mobile homes have accounted for about 15 percent of the nation's private housing production and just over 25 percent of detached-house construction. This is housing for buyers on tight budgets. Were it not for mobile homes, many people would be unable to own their homes—or would be living in run-down or unfinished housing.

Rural America especially has seized on the mobile home as an answer to its housing needs. Thirty years ago you could drive through the countryside and find people living in houses that consisted of nothing more than a basement; people would build a foundation, give it a rudimentary covering to keep out the rain, and live below ground level in a kind of concrete-block fortress with little natural light until they'd accumulated enough money to construct the first-floor quarters. Often, they'd remain in that crudely covered basement for years. Today, such depressing sights have disappeared from most of rural America. The "trailer" has grown up into today's better-equipped, more comfortable "mobile home." And as the mobile home has gotten larger and more generously outfitted, more and more people with limited finances—and some who are attracted by low-maintenance living—have moved into one of these "coaches," as some owners call them. (The industry succeeded in having the federal government designate its product as "manufactured housing," which is a disservice to the public, since that term already applied to modular housing—also produced in factories, but with a different and stronger method of construction. "Mobile homes" may not be mobile very often, but at least the term is one that everyone understands.)

Mobile homes cost only half as much per square foot as conventional houses built on their sites. For years, mobile homes had a reputation for being poorly insulated, for offering inadequate protection against severe storms, and, worst of all, for being firetraps. The Housing and Community Development Act of 1974 brought mobile homes under federal regulation, greatly alleviating many of their flaws. Fire-retardant materials have been adopted. Increasingly, instead of paneling, which can help flames spread, mobile homes are using gypsumboard for some of their interior surfaces. Insulation and protection against drafts have improved. In northern Indiana, one of the centers of mobile-home manufacturing, some companies build exterior walls 6 rather than 4 inches thick to offer better energy efficiency, with an R-value of 19.

"Double-wide" mobile homes (24–28 feet wide and 48–76 feet long) have done a good job of duplicating the floor plans of conventional houses. Many have spacious living rooms with vaulted ceilings and an open interior atmosphere. On the outside, some are difficult to distinguish from conventional homes. About two-thirds of the units today continue to take the customary long and narrow mobile home shape, but even these are adopting such characteristics of conventional houses as horizontal clapboardlike siding and pitched roofs covered with asphalt-composition shingles. Mobile homes clearly are becoming increasingly houselike.

The problems of mobile homes, however, have yet to be fully solved. People who are sen-

sitive to formaldehyde fumes may suffer from living in these dwellings, which are constructed with materials that emit them. And structurally, mobile homes may never attain the sturdiness of conventional houses. At Hawthorne, in Leesburg, Florida, retired people live in an attractive, well-planned community composed entirely of mobile homes, but one peculiarity visitors are quick to notice is that the owners place their washers and dryers in an enclosed structure under the carport, not inside the house. They don't want to shake the "coaches." Even the Manufactured Housing Institute, which represents the mobile-home manufacturers, acknowledges that there can be problems in strong winds if the units are not properly anchored. About thirty states have installation standards, notes Frank Walters, a technical specialist at the institute, and "not all do a good job of enforcing them."

What's needed is some spur to get the industry to move faster toward upgraded quality. In 1970, the talented architect Daniel Scully, after finishing his training at Yale University and completing a year of study abroad with a prestigious Prix de Rome fellowship, went to Indiana, heartland of the mobile-home industry, and tried to get work in the industry as a designer. The industry gave him the cold shoulder. This sort of obliviousness to design skill is still all too prevalent. Many manufacturers continue turning out mobile homes not only with the problems already cited but also with a general awkwardness—their roof edges either too thin or too fat, their windows unrelated in size or shape to one another. It's time the industry followed the lead of some of America's better

OVERLEAF
Mobile homes along a lake in Hawthorne—a 300-acre Leesburg, Florida, retirement community.

tract-housing developers, hiring outsiders who can improve the designs. The mobile home is going to be around for a long time, and it could become much more appealing.

Factory-production methods have achieved better results, both esthetically and structurally, with modular housing. Approximately 200 companies operate modular-home factories in the United States. Typically, they turn out hundreds of large, boxlike components (called "modules"), and two or more modules are joined at the homesite to make a house, which sits on a permanent foundation like a conventional site-built house. Roughly 95 percent of the construction work is completed before the modules leave the factory.

To make sure that modular sections can withstand being hauled over highways, factories customarily use more than one method of fastening. Walls are glued as well as nailed. Nails are grooved around their shanks to prevent them from pulling loose. Some sections are secured with metal stitchplates—flat rectangular pieces of metal with dozens of sharp projections that bite into a piece of wood and hold firm. In strength, modular houses generally are comparable to site-built houses. They can also achieve impressive energy efficiency. In periods when there's a healthy enough housing market to keep the factories busy, modular can be a more efficient and economical method of construction—free from delays caused by weather or by the difficulty of getting the right materials and tradespeople to the building site at the right time. Construction proceeds as a series of tightly coordinated steps, refined for maximum productivity. The same tasks are performed in the same sequence again and again. It's an assembly-line operation, and employees—feeling the pressure of much closer observation than do workers at dispersed homebuilding sites

—learn to work fast and effectively. If the factory establishes competent quality-control procedures, mistakes are quickly discovered, and the work attains a more consistent level of quality than that of houses built in the field.

Rural areas and small towns, commanding less access to homebuilding supplies and expertise, have long proven receptive to modular housing. More recently, modular housing has entered the cities, even New York's devastated South Bronx. The main reason is simple: the houses go up fast, leaving thieves and vandals less opportunity to damage unfinished buildings or to steal materials. Some suburban contractors also have switched to modular components to avoid the difficulties of finding and coordinating the many trades involved in conventional house construction.

In the United States, three somewhat different approaches to modular construction have gained varying degrees of acceptance. One is the method used by Cardinal Industries, by far the country's largest modular manufacturer. Cardinal began manufacturing modules in Columbus, Ohio, in 1970 for apartment developments and later branched into construction of detached houses, Knights Inn motels, congregate housing complexes for the elderly, and office parks—all of these using the same 1-story, slope-roofed, 12-by-24-foot modules with only minor modifications. In all, more than 100,000 of these modules have been produced by Cardinal's growing number of factories in Maryland, Georgia, Florida, and Ohio.

The company's founder, Austin Guirlinger, realized early that if he used the same materials, the same dimensions, the same techniques over and over again, Cardinal would enjoy economies of scale. By purchasing regularly in huge volumes, Cardinal could persuade suppliers to deliver materials in their most efficient form—eliminating some of the work that would otherwise have to be done in the company's factories. In Cardinal plants, no buzz saws whine; the lumber arrives precut to Cardinal's specifications. The company can afford good plumbing fixtures because it buys them in great quantity and forgoes the packaging and adapter kits supplied to other builders. The company, which finds private investors for each of its apartment complexes but remains involved in their management, has become knowledgeable about how all its standardized components and fixtures work. Indeed, Cardinal has developed its system so well that it issues each homeowner a manual explaining the operation of the heating and other systems, and it provides a complimentary "master parts kit" containing a bundle of roofing, a faucet-repair kit, two heating elements for the electric range, a 3-by-6-foot section of carpeting, 3 quarts of stain, 12 feet of base molding, and more than a half-dozen other items.

One of the keys to Cardinal's success as a modular-housing manufacturer has been its ability to spot promising untapped markets. Guirlinger recognized, for instance, that there was a shortage of modern apartments in many small towns—a scarcity that developers of site-built housing were not addressing. Cardinal concentrated on that niche in the housing market, and today Ohio, Indiana, Florida, and a few other states are liberally sprinkled with the firm's virtually identical complexes of sixty to seventy ground-floor apartments—complexes big enough to offer the services of a resident manager and small enough to feel noninstitutional. In these complexes, a single module forms a studio apartment containing a Murphy bed near the front and a kitchen and bathroom at the rear. Two modules make a one-bedroom apartment; three modules, a two-bedroom apartment. In many common-wall housing developments, sound travels from one unit to another, but modular construction helps to prevent that. Each module arrives with its own exterior walls, deadening sound somewhat, and then the modules are arranged back to back and with their sides next to one another—but with an enclosed 1-inch air space between units to block noise further.

Because the modular construction method allows costs to be reliably figured in advance, projects stay within their budgets. Often developers of conventionally constructed housing find their costs outrunning their estimates, and when they do, they end up scrimping on the last items in the budget, especially landscaping. But Cardinal, by avoiding budget overruns, is able to keep its landscaping up to a uniform standard. Each finished project has grass, trees, flowers, and other plantings. For every module —in other words, for every 12 feet of apartment frontage—$450 is spent on landscaping.

The modular method also gives buyers of a Cardinal detached house the advantage of starting with a small, affordable house that they know will easily accommodate future additions. The basic 864-square-foot dwelling consists of three modules placed side by side: one module containing the living and dining areas; the second containing the kitchen and a bedroom; and the third containing a bathroom, utility room, and another bedroom. When the occupants can afford more, they can add a master-bedroom-and-bathroom module to one end of the house, or they can attach a family-room module to the rear. They can also attach a two-car garage, also available from the company. These options are integral parts of the house design.

The biggest drawback to the Cardinal system is the inflexibility of its apartment designs. Although the apartments provide popular features such as ground-floor living, doors opening directly to the outdoors, and nearby parking— amenities that are absent from apartment complexes designed by some of the country's best architects—the modules' back-to-back placement eliminates cross-ventilation. So strongly does the company insist on avoiding deviations from standard procedure that even when an apartment is an end unit, the company refuses to put side windows in it.

And although Cardinal's housing is strong and snug, no one is likely to find the interiors inspirational. Ceilings are sprayed on. Interior walls are surfaced with vinyl coverings. The juncture of ceiling and wall is dressed up with molding, but the molding doesn't meet at the corners of the room: that would require the precise angle of a miter joint, and Cardinal doesn't want to be bothered with such precision in something so strictly decorative. Instead, Cardinal has resorted to an expedient—closing the gap at the corner with a brown rectangular plastic block that unconvincingly mimics wood. It's just a minor matter, but it's the sort of detail the eye automatically settles on. The clunky little plastic block aptly symbolizes a host of esthetic compromises in modular construction—a lack of the personal involvement and pride in details that enliven a really satisfying house.

Most modular housing producers have differed with Cardinal's rigid approach to standardization and favor an alternative that offers buyers a much greater variety of size, shape, and style. They've produced ranch houses, two-story Colonials, two-story townhouses, three-story apartment projects—a range of housing that continues to grow as the manufacturers master more complex designs. In contrast to Cardinal's insistence on turning out thousands of virtually identical modules, most other manufacturers have been willing to tailor their products somewhat to different buyers. Their flexibility has been rewarded (although in truth, Cardinal's method has been rewarded, too).

ABOVE
Modular production in a Cardinal Industries plant.
OPPOSITE TOP
An expandable Cardinal modular house.
OPPOSITE BOTTOM
Partly modular, partly site-built house by Heritage Homes in Costa Mesa, California.

Modular production has been gradually growing and now accounts for some 60,000 housing units a year.

Because the most efficient, transportable shape for a modular unit is rectilinear, there are limits to the design freedom currently available with most modular components. To overcome the constraints, some builders have tried a third approach to modular—using the inexpensively produced, quickly assembled modular sections for kitchens, bathrooms, and bedrooms and taking advantage of conventional methods to add elements with more drama, such as sunken living rooms with vaulted ceilings and roofs with interesting, complex shapes. Though modular

companies, intent on holding costs down, have kept the finishes and trim relatively Spartan, builders can overcome the esthetic meagerness by adding decorative elements like oak stair rails and stained-glass windows. Heritage Homes, in Costa Mesa, California, has used this hybrid kind of construction—60 percent modular, 40 percent site-built—to produce stylish houses with a more attractive level of finish. Designers such as Danielian Associates of Newport Beach, California, also have combined modular with site-built additions, striking a balance between economical construction and esthetic satisfaction. While the Cardinal approach offers great potential for strictly cost-conscious housing, a mixture of modular and site-built features could meet the needs of people who can afford something more generously finished.

For some Americans, none of these is the right approach. A remarkably different course has been charted by a number of individuals and companies interested in both a much higher quality of materials and more traditional method of construction. Since the late 1960s, there's been a growing backlash against mediocre craftsmanship and unimpressive construction. One expression of this has been the revival of the log house. When New England Log Homes was founded in 1969, it was one of a handful of log-house producers. Today it is a leading member of an industry composed of more than 250 companies. Estimates of log-house construction vary widely—from 20,000 to 40,000 a year—in part because log-house production is not restricted to large business organizations. An undetermined number of handcrafters and small companies also produce log houses in numbers not regularly tallied by any agency or association.

The resurgence of log houses owes much of its strength to the fact that they can be sold as kits that the purchaser assembles, saving a considerable amount of money. Many people have moved to rural areas in the past twenty years, and what looks as well suited to a woodsy setting as a house of logs? The log house has more going for it, though, than its back-to-the-land ambience and its status as the ultimate do-it-yourself project. The log house is impressively solid—its sturdiness proclaimed by walls up to 10 inches thick. Its materials are genuine and its appearance consistent, with the logs serving not only as structural elements but also as visible surfaces, inside as well as out. Gypsum-board walls can be installed on the interior, but the last thing most log-house owners want is walls composed of a factory-made product. Typically, the appeal of rustic wood pervades the whole house.

At the same time that the log-house revival was beginning, a number of people scattered throughout rural New England started returning to timber-frame construction, which relies on heavy posts and beams rather than two-by-four studwalls to frame the house. Post-and-beam construction had shown up in some California contemporary houses in the 1950s and 1960s, but the New England revival took its inspiration instead from the buildings erected in the Northeast in the seventeenth, eighteenth, and nineteenth centuries. Yankee Barn, Maine Post & Beam, and other companies arose to produce houses with thick, sturdy timbers. Maine Post & Beam, for instance, builds its houses with native Eastern or Northern white pine posts and beams that typically measure 6 inches by 6 inches. The summer beam supporting the center of the house measures 6 by 12 inches, and floor joists and rafters generally measure 4 inches wide and 8 or 10 inches high.

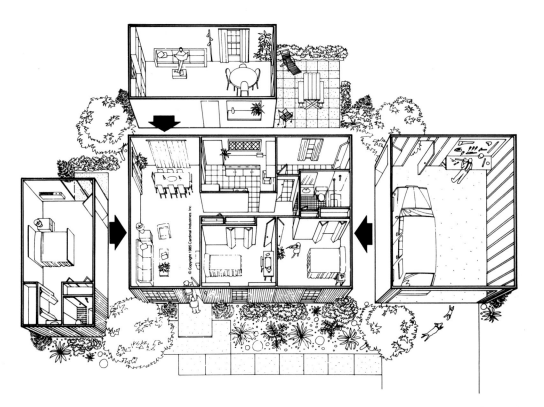

Plan showing how additional modules can later be added to a three-module, 864-square-foot Cardinal Industries house.

Yankee Barn uses lumber with similarly ample dimensions but obtains it from old New England buildings that are being torn down —mainly nineteenth-century warehouses and commercial structures. Timbers from the old buildings are resawn, notched, drilled, and numbered so that they can systematically be assembled at the new homesite. By using old timbers, Yankee Barn is able to get a species that's rare today—longleaf pine, which, according to one study, is about 80 percent heavier and stronger than white pine, a kind of wood often used in residential construction.

Methods of joining the posts and beams vary from one builder to another. Yankee Barn, for instance, cuts notches into the posts and into some of the beams to hold the structure in place on the posts. The company also uses heavy nails to further secure the frame. Maine Post & Beam simplifies the construction procedure by setting the beams on top of the posts and connecting them with wooden gusset plates and 1-inch-diameter oak pegs. In the intervals between the posts and beams along the perimeter walls, the company inserts two-by-six studwalls that are packed with fiberglass insulation and covered with gypsumboard. Some companies, however, take pride in hewing more closely to traditional methods. Timberpeg, of Claremont, New Hampshire, emphasizes that, unlike some other post-and-beam companies, its work crews do not use metal fasteners; instead Timberpeg relies on mortise-and-tenon joints. The tenon, a projection at the end of a timber, extends into a **153**

TOP
A house by Yankee Barn.
ABOVE
A Maine Post & Beam residence.
LEFT
*A Timberpeg house in southern Vermont, designed by
architect Lyman S. A. Perry.*

155

Walls and ceiling of Eastern white pine, finished with a semi-transparent white stain, in the Timberpeg house by Lyman S. A. Perry.

mortise, or slot; a peg is hammered in to hold the joint firmly.

Some companies, most of them considerably smaller, use still more elaborately traditional methods of timber framing. One of the best known traditional timber framers is Tedd Benson, owner of Benson Woodworking Company in Alstead Center, New Hampshire, and author, with James Gruber, of *Building the Timber Frame House*. Benson's goal is nothing less than the perpetuation of fine woodworking traditions of hundreds of years ago, when the best buildings not only were framed with posts and beams secured by notches, wooden braces, and mortise-and-tenon joints but also exhibited delicate detailing that made the frame an object of artistry.

There are roughly 250 timber-frame companies like Benson's—enterprises that remain small because their complex traditional joinery requires meticulous skilled workmanship. Connections must be precise to $1/32$ of an inch so that the tenon fits tightly into the mortise. "We use modern tools where we can," says Benson, "but it gets to the point where you have to pick up a mallet and chisel and finish it in the time-honored way." Many of the posts, beams, and braces are chamfered, a technique that miraculously transforms ponderous structural parts into elegant elements. Braces in Benson's houses take on graceful curves. Structure and ornament are one—not in frequently harsh materials such as steel and concrete, which architectural Modernists once glorified, but in wood, which possesses inherent warmth and appeal. Timber-frame houses are among the finest homes now being built in the United States. It's exhilarating to see handsome New Hampshire red oak being used not just for surface effect but for solid-looking structure. An increasingly critical attitude toward modern materials and methods has helped to popularize this throwback to venerable building practices, but Benson contends that acceptance of the timber-frame house "is not earned on the winds of nostalgia; the craftsmanship of man is critical to the value and integrity of the buildings we live in. One of the mistakes in the application of production technology to home construction has been the simultaneous reduction of quality standards and reduction in the use of natural materials."

All the varieties of post-and-beam construction—whether they use traditional joinery alone or compromise with somewhat more modern procedures—allow great freedom for interior design, since the load is carried by widely spaced posts and there is no need for interior bearing walls. In the home of Ray and Nancy Holmes in York, Maine, built by Maine Post & Beam, the entire first floor on the south side is open—from the kitchen on the eastern end, through the skylighted dining room in the center, to the living room on the west. In central Connecticut, a house that Benson built for Mark and Fran Ludwig has an 18-by-23-foot living room that soars two and a half stories. Up three steps from the living room—and visible beyond Benson's delicately carved golden timbers—are the dining room and kitchen of the spacious and largely open first floor. Such openness can lend itself not only to dramatic architectural effects and modern living patterns but also to the most efficient use of radiant heat; a growing number of people in rural sections of the country heat their homes with a wood stove, and an open interior allows the warmth to circulate much more easily.

In earlier times, the space between posts along the perimeter of a timber-frame house would have been filled in with brick, plaster, or other materials to provide some protection from outdoor conditions. Today much better alternatives exist. Benson typically covers the exterior of his houses with "stress-skin panels"—sandwichlike rectangular panels that contain gypsumboard on the interior side, 3½ inches of rigid-foam insulation in the core, and waferboard on the outside. The exterior clapboards, shingles, or other covering goes over the stress-skin panel. Consequently the frame remains completely visible on the interior while being shielded from condensation and weather. The structure can survive indefinitely. "We start," Benson says, "with the concept that we're going to build something that will last 300, 400, 500 years."

Of the nearly 2 million housing units constructed in the United States in a good year, probably 3,000 or so are traditional timber-frame houses like Benson's. Another 7,000 or so are post-and-beam houses in which the joinery is simplified, metal or fiberglass fasteners are used, and, in some cases, the posts and beams are not the sole means of structural support. Small though the numbers may be, they are on the increase. Timberpeg, for instance, started in Vermont in 1974 and now operates factories in New Hampshire, Colorado, and North Carolina. The number of timber-frame and post-and-beam houses may never rival that

RIGHT, TOP TO BOTTOM
Houses by Tedd Benson in central Connecticut; in Salem, New York; and in Ashburnham, Massachusetts. All are passive solar designs.
OPPOSITE
A timber-frame house by Maine Post & Beam in York River Farms, York, Maine.

LEFT
Carpenters, led by Len Brackett on ladder, raising a hari, *or log beam, for a Japanese-style house in Tiburon, California. A curve in the log beam is not unusual in Japanese construction, though this one is more pronounced than most.*

TOP
Copper roof shingles being crimped so that they will interlock.

ABOVE
Roof shingles being installed.

161

TOP

Sliding windows in Brackett's Tiburon house.

ABOVE

A sunlit Japanese bathing tub, or ofuro.

RIGHT

Translucent screens cast a glow on wooden surfaces.

OPPOSITE

162 *Living room with floor of black ash.*

of conventionally constructed housing, but these old forms of construction, with their marriage of beauty and solidity, are making their way across much of the country.

In the Southwest, the search for a strong, substantial kind of house has resulted in a revival of adobe-style construction. In a few other places around the country, it has led to much more exotic solutions. A house can represent whatever culture, whatever height of craftsmanship the builder brings to it. One of the most remarkable examples of a builder's belief in the importance of craftsmanship is a residence completed in 1986 by Len Brackett. In 1970, Brackett went to Japan, where he fell in love with the temples of Kyoto, the old imperial capital. He soon found work as an apprentice to Japanese temple builders—the elite of that country's carpenters. For 6 years, Brackett often spent 80 hours a week hand-planing wood and learning the ways of these supremely meticulous craftsmen. After returning to the United States, he set up a shop northeast of Sacramento, high in the foothills of the Sierra Nevadas, and built his family a Japanese house.

In the shop, Brackett and two partners later began fabricating a house for sale, taking pains to achieve the utmost quality. They obtained logs of a few carefully selected species—sugar pine, redwood, Port Orford cedar (an especially fragrant cypress), and some American chestnut that had escaped the blight of several decades ago and died only recently. They had the logs milled into six-by-twelves and then dried the wood for two to three years. They sawed the wood into the dimensions they needed and finished it with precise Japanese hand tools, including planes capable of shaving the wood as thin as a thousandth of an inch. To ensure absolute accuracy in cutting, they put lines on the wood with a *sumitsubo*—a writing instrument that uses India ink—and a *sumisashi,* an inkpot that can be used with a fine string to produce a marking more minute and exact than the carpenter's customary lead pencil or chalk line. The ink doesn't penetrate; it remains on the surface, coming off with a sweep of the plane.

For nearly four years, Brackett and his partners made the wooden parts of the house. Then they loaded them into a tractor-trailer and transported them some 150 miles to Tiburon, just north of San Francisco in Marin County. There, in September 1985, they began putting the parts together with intricate joinery. The result is a 2,800-square-foot house with Japanese character and carpentry, but with features suited to American living. Interlocking copper shingles cover its roof. The floor is black ash—handsome yet tough enough that people can wear shoes inside without harming it. The house contains a Japanese bathroom with a cypress tub, but it also has two full American-style bathrooms, along with four bedrooms. Perhaps the most spectacular feature is its light. Throughout the house, Brackett laminated plane shavings of western red cedar—$^1/_{1000}$ to $^3/_{1000}$ of an inch thick—to the glass of the lighting fixtures. When the fixture is turned off, it looks like wood. When it's switched on, it produces a wonderful warm illumination.

Brackett's Japanese carpentry is a particularly dramatic example of what appears to be a growing awareness of the importance of craftsmanship. One leading impetus toward the recovery and revival of fine building traditions was the historic preservation movement that emerged during the 1970s and came to focus more and more people's admiration on the qualities of old houses—on their finishes and details as well as their architectural form. In some cases, the demand for people skilled in making reproductions and replacement parts for old buildings gave rise to enterprises that later allotted most of their services to new housing. In Westminster, Vermont, for instance, the Woodstone Company was founded in 1978, concentrating on producing handcrafted wooden windows and doors, many of them in hard-to-get nonrectangular shapes. About half were for old buildings being restored or rehabilitated. "We came in at just the right time, with the boom in historic preservation and the interest in having 'real' things, not plastic things," said Richard Chamberland, vice-president of Woodstone, which has doubled its production nearly every year in the 1980s.

Woodstone insisted on making windows and doors with authentic detailing, based not on rough approximations of old styles but rather, in many instances, on a particular window or door that a customer wanted to reproduce. Woodstone custom-ground its knives so that it could carve wood to match the profile, for example, of old fanlights, arched windows, double-hung windows with true divided lights, and windows with curved moldings creating a spider-web effect, all of which were built with strong, traditional mortise-and-tenon joints. In just a few years, however, the demand for such elements in new construction has grown so much that four-fifths of Woodstone's products now go into brand-new buildings; some large window makers, also sensing the opportunity for individually designed windows, have also decided to offer custom fabrication.

Companies and craftsmen responding to the enthusiasm for stained and leaded glass in old buildings are now producing an enormous variety of decorative stained and leaded glass for windows and doors in new houses, often with a clear second pane of glass added for insulating value. Just as Tedd Benson has succeeded in wedding traditional timber-framing techniques to the latest in rigid-foam insulating technology, many other artisans have tried to incorporate modern advances unobtrusively into their products. Woodstone, for instance, makes beautiful carved, paneled doors in pine, mahogany, cherry, and oak with a core of rigid-foam insulation, delivering an R-value of 5.

———

Today there's a booming trade in such decorative elements as handmade tiles, which many homeowners install in their kitchens, often on the walls above the stove or between the base and wall cabinets. In Stamford, Connecticut, for instance, Karen Kalkstein makes custom-designed tiles, some in a "quilt pattern" depicting a family's history, some portraying favorite animals or the landscape surrounding the house, others illustrating fruits and flowers.

Craftsmanship also finds expression in new forms and modern materials. Increasingly people are seizing the artistic potential of synthetic substances in kitchens and bathrooms. Designers are fashioning the Formica Corporation's ColorCore into sleek, sculptural counters, tables, vanities, and other components with curves, ziggurats, and rounded, beveled, or chamfered edges. Individuals experienced in home construction and remodeling enjoy discovering new possibilities of materials like Avonite, DuPont Corian, and Formica Brand 2000X—nonporous, solid materials that are easy to work with, since they can be sawn, drilled or routed, embellished with inlays, and molded into a variety of shapes. As Jeffrey Locke, a skilled carpenter in New Haven, Connecticut, observes of Corian, "people can live out their fantasies with it. It's such a flexible product, you're limited only by what you can think to do with it."

Companies such as Focal Point, Inc., of Atlanta use synthetic materials like high-density polyurethane to produce moldings extraordinarily faithful to the designs of centuries ago. One of the few liberties that Focal Point takes with the original patterns is, for instance, to reduce the scale slightly for cornice moldings going into houses with ceilings lower than those in old houses. There, the original moldings wouldn't have looked quite right.

New houses are emulating many of the esthetic features of houses from the past. A few architects, like Allan Greenberg in New Haven, have launched a serious revival of classical architecture, investing great care in the houses' craftsmanship and detailing. A larger number of designers have gravitated to old forms and features and used them more loosely, even whimsically. In downtown Chicago, the architectural firm of Weese Hickey Weese designed a new apartment tower, Chestnut Place, and commissioned the trompe l'oeil artist Richard Haas to paint its lobby to resemble the interior of San Miniato al Monte, a Romanesque church in Florence, Italy. In a house in Door County, Wisconsin, the Chicago architectural firm of Nagle, Hartray & Associates designed the wall around a fireplace to be built of logs and mortar, with the ends of the logs protruding into the room—a variation on the "stovewood" construction that the inhabitants of that rural area used a century or more ago, when short logs were employed in house additions, usually with the log ends covered by plaster. Architects have rediscovered such old-time materials as wood lattice and are using them once again to ornament houses and grounds. Some architects recently have even carved sculptural shapes out of materials as humble as gypsumboard.

Natural materials can give a house a stirring spirit, the kind of vitality exemplified by the houses that Norman Jaffe, a Bridgehampton, New York, architect, is acclaimed for designing near the seashore at the eastern end of Long Island. Jaffe gives his houses strong, dynamic shapes. "The little building is an annoyance on God's vast landscape," he asserts. He plays the hardness of stone walls, fireplaces, and floors against the softer textures of wood walls, roofs, and ceilings. "I try to remember," he says, "that I'm designing with the light. I've gotten up before sunrise to watch the light on a house. It's such a miracle. The light on the rough-sawn pine makes the shadows strong."

In the best designs, materials are matched to their regions and settings. In Arizona, sensible builders avoid using wood on exteriors. The sharp contrast between the dehydrating heat of the harsh desert sun and the soaking August monsoons too often causes it to buckle. Stucco serves better. Most builders in the Southwest today give the stucco a rough texture; it's the easy thing to do. But some architects, such as George W. Christensen in Phoenix, take pains to produce stucco with a smooth, sand-float finish, which is more elegant, even if fine lines appear on its surface. Christensen tries to achieve the solidly three-dimensional feeling associated with early buildings in the Southwest. Walls with no openings in them are built about 7 inches thick, but where there are windows and doors, Christensen adds to the wood framing under the stucco exterior until the walls are 12–24 inches thick. With such deep walls, windows can have wide sills on both the inside and the outside, making the house feel richer and more protective.

The Straus house—designed by O'Neill Conrad Oppelt Architects of San Antonio for ranchland west of that city—has much the same three-dimensional character. The walls of the Straus house consist of stucco applied over a double

Floral pattern in bathroom wall tiles by Karen Kalkstein.

thickness of concrete block; it captures the feeling of southern Texas's historic adobe buildings but offers more permanence than genuine adobe —a soft, muddy material that washes away in the rain. Fine attention to detail and materials is evident throughout this home. Stacked blocks of limestone support the main beam between the living and dining areas. Trusses made of solid timbers hold up the pitched ceiling of pine in the living room. Floors are covered in locally made tile. Doors are made of vertical wood slats and are equipped with old-style box locks —big black locks that require a large key. Every part of the house has been crafted to produce a building that's exquisite in its details as well as alluring in its overall design.

For a number of years, there's been a widespread belief that old skills cannot be found anymore and that craftsmanship is inevitably on the way out of American houses. This is largely a misconception based on the trend toward increasingly industrialized, time-saving materials and procedures in tract homebuild- **167** ing. In reality, materials and detailing of great beauty continue to be used, and not exclusively in the most expensive houses. Good tilework shows up in many houses in the Southwest. In Arizona, tiles even form decorative bands on the exteriors of new attached houses, making a pleasing contrast against the expanses of tan stucco. In many parts of the country, decorative woodwork is increasingly available, indoors and out. Some kinds of craftsmanship, such as plastering, are much rarer than in the past, and yet many of the "disappearing" trades can still be found if people want them.

One of the valuable things that's happened in the past couple of decades has been the proliferation of local and regional preservation groups — useful sources of information about where to find good materials and tradespeople. Another positive development has been the growth of magazines, such as *Fine Homebuilding* and *The Old-House Journal,* that provide a convenient way to tap into sources of high-quality material and craftsmanship for use in both new and old houses. Still another beneficial development has been the establishment of workshops that provide instruction for people who want to build or act as contractor for their own houses. Currently, some forty owner-builder schools around the country give people hands-on construction experience. At least one school — Yestermorrow in Warren, Vermont — devotes most of a two-week course to design, helping the students devise floorplans that fit the way they live. Probably the best source of information on owner-builder programs is *Home Resource* magazine, published in Boulder, Colorado. A little bit of sleuthing may be needed to find some of the elements that give a house the personality its owner is looking for. There are, however, a lot of informal networks among preservationists, architects, and artisans that can help to locate these features. The well-crafted house has by no means become an extinct or even an endangered species. It takes effort to get a house with imaginative design, solid construction, and beautiful surfaces, but, in truth, it's always been so.

OPPOSITE
A wall of Delaware golden-veined stone supports an oak ceiling in a Southampton, New York, house designed by Norman Jaffe. The floor is of Tennessee paving stone.

Chapter Five

Old Buildings, Modern Uses

A bright and inventive house designed by Cambridge, Massachusetts, architect Graham Gund rises from what had been a two-car garage in Boston's Beacon Hill neighborhood.

171

In the past two decades, historic preservation has blossomed into a mass movement affecting not just the San Franciscos, Charlestons, and Bostons of the nation but also many less celebrated places in between—places where old architecture was less renowned but nonetheless merited saving. For a country accustomed to equating "new" with "better," this was a major change, and it took years of effort to persuade the public that old buildings deserve protection and care.

In many cities, skeptical financial institutions had to be convinced that investing in restoration and rehabilitation made sense. In the early 1960s, for instance, New York City banks were so leery of Brooklyn's Park Slope neighborhood that when Everett Ortner, an editor at *Popular Science,* and his wife, Evelyn, an interior designer, decided to buy one of the sturdy but neglected four-story brownstones there, a dozen banks turned down their mortgage application before one finally agreed to lend them the money.

The ensuing years saw a remarkable transformation in that nineteenth-century neighborhood. If bankers once looked askance at people heading for Park Slope, today they tend to look on them with envy, for the area, which sits adjacent to the curving paths of 526-acre Prospect Park, abounds with richly detailed brownstones that have been lovingly renovated or restored. Brooklyn's brownstones gradually emerged as prime examples of the charm of historic neighborhoods—this during a long period in which Everett Ortner devoted his nonediting hours to working as an urban architectural missionary, helping organize first the Park Slope Betterment Committee, next the citywide Brownstone Revival Committee, and, in 1974, a national neighborhood-preservation organization called Back to the City, Inc.

Encouraged by the Ortners, many others saw the potential of dingy but eminently reclaimable old buildings, and Brooklyn has experienced the welcome revival of many of its brownstone neighborhoods—among them Fort Greene, Carroll Gardens, Clinton Hill, Cobble Hill, Boerum Hill, even parts of tough Bedford-Stuyvesant. Not that all of these names would be familiar to a longtime Brooklynite. Cobble Hill and Carroll Gardens had previously been known by the less alluring names of South Brooklyn and Red Hook. Clinton Hill, to some Brooklynites, was just an undifferentiated section of Bedford-Stuyvesant (and to some of its inhabitants, it still is).

The unspoken premise is: if you can bestow a pleasant-sounding name on a square mile or so that otherwise would have been awash in urban anonymity, the neighborhood will be more attractive to renovators and restorers. The new name can help define an area and encourage a sense of community; if the new name also looks good in the Sunday real estate section, so much the better.

Throughout the nation, old houses with architectural character have been made fresh again. Baltimore's old Federal Hill has undergone major rehabilitation, some of it from urban homesteaders who bought abandoned houses for $1 each. Washington's run-down Capitol Hill has similarly been restored. In San Antonio, old houses in the King William district have been renewed. On the North Side of Pittsburgh, the red brick houses on the "Mexican War streets," so called because they were named for the war's battlefields and generals, have undergone renovation. This trend has affected some portion of probably every sizable city in the United States.

Subsidies, tax incentives, and other special

Back to the City, Inc.

The Boone house in Springfield, Massachusetts, after years of restoration.

programs have given preservation a boost, but the main reasons for it have been the architectural quality of old houses, the space they provide in contrast with new houses, their close-in locations, and—at the beginning of a neighborhood's comeback—their low prices. The typical brownstone offers about 1,000 square feet per floor—roughly 4,000 square feet in a four-story house, as compared to a total of about 1,600 square feet in the typical American single-family detached house built today. The brownstone revival organizers in the 1960s and 1970s used the slogan "Twice the house for half the money." That may no longer be true for brownstones in today's most sought-after locations, such as Park Slope or Manhattan's Upper West Side, where houses that sold for $15,000 to

$30,000 in the mid-1960s now sell for $500,000 to $1 million, but it still applies to many old houses across the country. Most preservation remains a matter of individuals or families acting on one house at a time, predominantly with their own money and often with much of their own labor. In parts of Boston's South End, in the Mount Adams area of Cincinnati, in Summit Hill in St. Paul, in Angeleno Heights in Los Angeles, and in other neighborhoods around the country, thousands of derelict buildings have been put back in good condition through years of work by their inhabitants.

Some states, such as Massachusetts, have seen an especially strong revival of old buildings. A striking example of the work that's flourished in recent years is Jim and Merry Boone's **173** restoration of a twelve-room Queen Anne–style house in Springfield, Massachusetts. Jim Boone, a high-school guidance counselor, had noticed the deteriorating house in 1974 on Florida Street, in a once-grand but long-decaying neighborhood a mile east of Springfield's downtown. Built in 1887, the house boasted a wealth of attractive features, including an octagonal corner tower, a front porch with elaborate wooden ornamentation, an expansive side porch, and a recessed third-floor balcony. For an urban site, the property was unusually spacious—a half-acre, complete with a two-story carriage barn. What most attracted Boone initially, however, were the windows—nearly a dozen of them stained-glass.

The Florida Street house had originally been a single-family dwelling, but by the time Boone saw it, it had been a boarding house for elderly tenants for more than thirty years, and it stood vacant for more than a year before the Boones were able to purchase it in the fall of 1976.

The Boones took advantage of some of the kinds of sources that other homeowners have used to carry out restoration projects. From the Springfield Historical Commission, they received a government-supplied $4,000 grant enabling them to hire a contractor to begin extensive exterior restoration—rebuilding the porches, repairing the gray slate roof, replacing deteriorated shingles and clapboard, and caring for the corner tower's neglected stonemasonry.

The Boones researched paint colors by examining photographs of local houses that were compiled in 1939 by the Works Progress Administration and by using a book distributed by Devoe Paint, *Exterior Decoration: Victorian Colors for Victorian Houses,* published in 1975 by the Athenaeum of Philadelphia. (This book continues to be sold or lent out by Devoe paint dealers. Other paint companies also sell guides

174

ABOVE, TOP TO BOTTOM
The Boone house's front foyer, front parlor, and stained glass in a foyer door.
OPPOSITE
Front parlor with original stained glass and a hand-silkscreened wall covering in a late-nineteenth-century pattern.

to historic painting schemes. One of the most highly regarded is *A Century of Color,* by Roger Moss, published in 1981 by the American Life Foundation in Watkins Glen, New York. Available at some Sherwin-Williams Company outlets, it's a guide to house paint colors from 1820 to 1920, complete with color illustrations of houses reproduced from nineteenth-century paint books and with sample cards of historic paint colors that are still being produced.)

When the Boones bought their home, its exterior walls and trim were a single shade of dark brown, which had been peeling for years. Like a growing number of old-house owners, they chose a more lively, variegated composition — pale brown for the body of the house, dark brown for the trim, and sage green for decorative accents on the porch and for a band of fish-scale shingles that wraps around the house between the clapboard siding of the first and second stories. The tendency today is to use paint to draw attention to a historic house's often-profuse detailing. In many cities, local preservation organizations and Neighborhood Housing Services offices encourage this trend by offering advice on paint colors and sometimes awarding prizes for the best work that's historically fitting.

The Florida Street house didn't have even one storm window, so, over several years, the Boones searched for wood-frame storm windows, eventually obtaining them for the entire house and for the carriage house. Inside, it took three years for the Boones to strip paint from wainscoting and other woodwork and to refinish the surfaces. Most people who restore or rehabilitate a house end up modernizing the

View from front parlor to back parlor. Frieze paper is a reproduction, in original colors, of a Theodore Dresser design from the 1880s.

177

kitchen and bathrooms, but this isn't the only conceivable approach. The Boones resolved to make the house as consistent as possible, so in the kitchen they refinished the wainscoting and the six doors (leading to three pantries, a back stairway, the basement, and the vestibule) and installed a tin ceiling. "You can still buy tin ceilings in sheets running maybe 4 by 8 feet," says Merry Boone. "They're from the original molds, from the same suppliers as at the turn of the century." The Boones complemented the kitchen's original soapstone sink by adding a Hoosier cabinet and vintage 1920s stove and refrigerator. In their quest for historical authenticity, they found an elevated oak tank, recovered from a Rhode Island dump, for an old-style high-tank toilet.

Through an advertisement, the Boones found an iron fence in Pennsylvania. They transported it to Massachusetts in 8-foot sections, then sandblasted the rust off of it and installed it to restore the traditional appearance of their grounds. Behind the fence, in the side yard, sits a cast iron fountain that they brought from Maine.

In 1982, the Boones told *The Old-House Journal:* "We are very settled in this magnificent house and look forward to a lifetime of satisfying projects here." And indeed, they have since added canvas awnings like those used on nineteenth-century houses, and they have applied period reproduction wallpapers to walls and to some of the ceilings, as had been done in elaborate houses of that period. In the back parlor, four different papers were placed on the ceiling. A series of six papers was installed on the dining-room ceiling. In the most formal room in the house, the front parlor, seven papers are now arranged in a pattern that radiates from a center rosette.

Since the Boones began restoring their house in Springfield, the services and sources of advice available to rehabbers and restorers have grown steadily in both quality and variety. *The Old-House Journal,* published in Brooklyn, won a devoted following from its first issue in 1973, and its content has improved over the years—no doubt reflecting not only the increasing expertise of its own staff, but also the growing professionalism of the historic-preservation field as a whole. Besides presenting product evaluations, how-to information, residential architectural history, and stories of individual projects—all in an informal style leavened with humor—the journal pungently expresses its opinions on the right and wrong things to do to a house (as in its illustrated "Remuddling of the Month"). For several years, it has published an annual catalogue of commercially available products and services; those that don't meet the journal's standards are excluded from its listings.

The National Trust for Historic Preservation also carries advice and advertising in its *Historic Preservation* magazine and ads in its newspaper, *Preservation News.* Many state and local preservation organizations provide guidance for rehabbers, sometimes compiling lists of contractors experienced in preservation specialties. Another source of information on technical issues, such as how to clean brick and stone exteriors, is a series of *Preservation Briefs,* published by the U.S. Department of the Interior.

Whereas people undertaking restoration projects once had to hunt intently for the architectural elements they needed, now their search is much easier. The number of companies listed in *The Old-House Journal's* catalogue has grown from 205 in 1976 to more than 1,400 today. Many stores and warehouses cater to the restorer's needs. Some concentrate on huge quantities of basic building components, such as old doors, while others specialize in a smaller number of showroom-quality items that have been cleaned and repaired. Some of these operations (listed in the phone book under "architectural salvage" or "architectural antiques") are organized into networks, such as Great American Salvage, which started in Montpelier, Vermont, and has since added affiliates in Manhattan; Sag Harbor, New York; New Haven, Connecticut; and Jacksonville, Florida. By getting in touch with one store, you can learn whether the piece you're looking for is available at any of the other branches. As networks begin to flourish, geographical constraints are waning. Observes Preston Maynard, of Great American Salvage's New Haven store: "You can send a fireplace mantel from Connecticut to Texas for $150."

There are also more tradesmen geared specifically to restoring or rehabilitating old buildings — repairing rotted Corinthian columns, putting plasterwork back in condition, or doing period-style housepainting. Rather than call any of them out of the blue (or out of the yellow pages, as the case may be), it's best to check first with a local preservation group or with architects who work on old buildings, since some artisans are experts in name only; some masonry "restorers," for instance, still do exterior sandblasting, even though it's been known for years that this practice destroys old brickwork.

Some preservation specialists prefer traditional methods and materials, but more alternatives become available all the time. Terracotta decorations are reproduced in glass-fiber-reinforced concrete, eighteenth-century cornice moldings are cast in lightweight, high-density polyurethane (which handles like yellow pine), and a host of new substitutions have been de-

vised for other items that used to be made from natural materials. The quality of these synthetic-based materials can be very high. For example, Focal Point, Inc., of Atlanta reproduces cornice moldings and chair rails accurately enough that they're authorized by the Colonial Williamsburg Foundation. Synthetics raise longstanding questions about truth in materials, but in many instances the new products are less costly than traditional craftsmanship and much easier to obtain.

———

As preservation has found a broader audience, some restoration projects have gotten larger, and so have developers — which can be good or bad. Unlike the individuals and couples who fix up old houses largely because they're drawn by architectural heritage, financial gain tends to loom largest in the minds of developers. An example of the high-quality rehabilitation carried out by the country's better developers is the revival of the eight-story Green Brier apartment building in Chicago by Landmark Properties, Inc., a locally based firm that was founded after the Tax Reform Act of 1981 granted tax incentives for work on historic structures.

Chicago architect Edmund Krause designed the Green Brier in 1903, imbuing it with the classical spirit that had become firmly embedded in American architecture by the beginning of the twentieth century. Located on West Surf Street in the city's Lakeview section, the Green Brier was nothing if not dignified. The tan Roman-brick building had a U-shaped plan that allowed the entrance to be placed more than 60 feet back from the street; the building's two wings extended forward to create a stately forecourt through which residents and visitors entered. Windows had classical lintels with distinctive projecting keystones, and inside, the lobby and the apartments were gen-

Court of Chicago's Green Brier apartment building with its templelike entrance.

erously proportioned.

After the Second World War, the Green Brier went into decline. The interior was split into smaller apartments, and much of the building's grandeur had dissipated by 1983, when Landmark Properties purchased both it and the Commodore, a similar apartment building directly across the street. Krause had designed both buildings, and when they were new they faced each other like decorous gentlemen dressed in formal attire. By 1986, when Landmark's work was complete, both buildings looked much as they had eighty years before. The entrance to the Green Brier is as grand as ever. The forecourt sits behind a black fence of wrought iron, and a pair of limestone pillars flanks the walkway to the entrance portico, where GREEN BRIER

is carved in limestone above the double doors.

In the lobby and halls, clay tile floors with a white diamond design on a dark terra-cotta-colored background have been restored, and the mahogany woodwork has regained its luster. Workers spent nearly a year stripping and refinishing wood surfaces throughout the building. Oak wainscoting adorns the living rooms of approximately half of the seventy-eight apartments. About half of the apartments also have pocket doors, with walnut facing the living room and oak facing the dining room. Other rooms are separated by doors of solid oak. The apartments, now sold as condominium units, have regained their former spaciousness. The living and dining rooms again look solidly traditional, with refinished oak baseboards more than a foot high, with thick compound moldings along 10–11-foot-high ceilings, and with refinished window and door trim 6–8 inches wide. As in many rehabilitated individual houses, the traditionalism recaptured in the living room, dining room, and bedrooms doesn't extend everywhere. Modernism prevails in the kitchen, where no attempt was made to re-create a turn-of-the-century appearance. All of the bathrooms are lined with new marble-tile walls and floors, however, that recall their original character.

One of the challenges of projects like the Green Brier is to satisfy modern energy-efficiency requirements without sacrificing historical and architectural integrity. The Green Brier typifies many buildings in National Register historic districts in that the developer was allowed to replace the windows not visible from the street—windows on the rear wall and on parts of the side walls—that, even when the building was new, had been less handsomely finished than those at the front. Original windows were retained in areas conspicuous from

Commodore apartment building, built in 1898 and renovated in the mid-1980s in concert with the Green Brier.   **181**

the street, and storm windows were installed on their interiors, leaving the street-side appearance unchanged.

Regulations affecting restoration and rehabilitation projects that receive public funds or that are located in registered historic districts have gotten more stringent over the years. Today the rules discourage such once-common practices as replacing the original windows with new ones possessing a different character. Anyone who's ever looked at the large sheets of glass that, in the 1970s, were often used to replace old-style windows can only be pleased by the tighter authenticity requirements. Windows are as crucial to a building's appearance as eyes are to the human face. If historic buildings are to be altered, the permissible changes are generally restricted to elements that don't disrupt the buildings' established personalities.

When a building is being converted to an entirely new use, however, it can be much more difficult to make the original features suit their new purposes. In the past two decades, many schools, churches, factories, and other nonresidential buildings have been turned into housing. It would be pleasant to report that the results have been uniformly successful, but the truth is, some of the conversions give a sense of having been forced. Schools, in particular, present the problem of what to do with broad hallways and big central auditoriums. An auditorium, even with its floor turned into a garden, may feel desolate, like a mall without any shoppers. Wide hallways designed for hundreds of noisy, exuberant students on their way to class feel *too* wide when they're populated by only a handful of tenants on their way quietly in and out. Churches, when they have tall stained-glass windows and massive sloping ceilings, can make it difficult to create practical apartment layouts and floor levels.

Ten years ago, Peter Blake, in his attack on modern architecture, *Form Follows Fiasco,* asserted, "All over the world, buildings that have been recycled from an earlier function to a new one seem to serve their users better today than they ever did before. . . ." This kind of sentiment was inevitable in the 1970s, when the destructive days of urban renewal were fresh in every preservationist's mind and conversions were a new phenomenon. Today a laudatory attitude is still more or less expected when discussing conversions (or "adaptive reuse," in the jargon of the preservation establishment). But by now, even ardent defenders of old buildings ought to be able to acknowledge that serious problems can result when the conversion work has to be held to a bare-bones budget or when the designer fails to recognize that original window openings, hall widths, and ceiling heights may be inconducive to a residential atmosphere.

The fact is, it often takes ingenuity and a substantial investment to fit housing into buildings that weren't intended for it. Sometimes people are so intent on saving a cherished building that they underestimate how much work is required to make it serve its new purposes well. While it's true that a certain number of people will endure a lot of discomforts simply to live in a building that has a history and an unusual personality, everyone should recognize that these buildings require a higher-than-average level of design talent and often need considerable alteration. Churches frequently need new windows in positions different from the old stained glass. Schools often need their public areas reduced to reasonable dimensions. Enthusiasm for saving a venerable building shouldn't blind us to the problems that a successful conversion must overcome.

Some of the nation's finest preservation projects are in Seattle, and two developments there illustrate divergent and effective ways of putting housing in turn-of-the-century school buildings. One, the former Interlake Elementary School, a three-story clapboard structure built in 1904, stands at a busy intersection in the Wallingford neighborhood's business district. Converting the building entirely to residential use was economically unfeasible, but the developer, Lorig Associates, saw that a mixture of retailing and residential uses held promise, especially since federally subsidized financing was available for the development of moderate-income apartments. Existing wide corridors running between entrances at both ends of the building meant that the first two floors could be lined with a series of commercial enterprises. A bookstore, a toy store, a restaurant, and other stores selling merchandise ranging from Caribbean clothes to kitchen items occupy much of what's now been christened the Wallingford Center. A high-quality specialty foods store moved into the school's old gymnasium.

The Wallingford Center's twenty-four apartments are all on the third floor, served by a set of the original staircases locked off at the residential floors so that shoppers don't wander up there. The original wide corridor wasn't needed on this floor, so Tonkin & Koch, architect of the conversion, found better uses for it. Part of its width was retained as a hall, but new walls were constructed that portioned some of its space into interiors for apartments. The apartments have a loft with about 6 feet of headroom above the bathroom and kitchen; some tenants use the loft for sleeping, others for an art studio. The kitchens, designed with a contemporary feeling, open up into living and dining areas, which have retained much of their old classroom character—with original doors, 13-foot ceilings, original 10-foot-high wooden windows, heavy trim, plaster walls and ceilings, and, in all but four apartments, refinished floors of maple or Douglas fir.

A few miles away, Seattle's West Queen Anne Elementary School (named for its neighborhood, not for the Queen Anne style) stands deep in a residential area, so commercial uses were out of the question; the entire building had to be converted to housing. To keep the old school grounds from being dominated by pavement and parked cars, the architect, Cardwell/ Thomas & Associates, turned an asphalt and concrete playground into a spacious front lawn and put most of the parking in a new garage underneath it. The firm carved forty-nine con-

"The School House" in Mechanicsburg, Pennsylvania, before its conversion to housing by Historic Landmarks for Living. Many schools sit in residential neighborhoods, and housing is frequently the only new use that is politically acceptable.

183

Wallingford Center in Seattle contains apartments on the top floor and two floors of retailing below. Interior view is of the shopping mall on the second level.

Four views of West Queen Anne School *(clockwise from top left):* a preserved entrance, a hall with new arches, a unit
in the former gymnasium, and another unit with original roundheaded window.

TOP
Public School 78 in Brooklyn, New York, with old maple flooring and 14-foot ceilings.
BELOW
Five-level apartment built around a stairwell of St. Mary's School in Troy, New York.

dominium apartments out of the Romanesque brick structure, which had been built in 1895 and successively added onto in 1899, 1902, and 1916. As at Wallingford Center, original windows were retained—here most of them were 5 by 8 feet—and the corridors were narrowed to create a more comfortable feeling and to make the apartments larger. Val Thomas, architect and project developer, put arches in hallway entrances as a further humanizing touch. Vertical fir wainscoting, maple floors, window trim, and wall moldings were preserved in the old classrooms. The original stairway and old lighting fixtures were also saved. The gymnasium—often the most difficult area to convert—became a large, skylighted, multilevel apartment for Thomas himself, complete with kitchen countertops made of blackboard slate.

In most preservation projects, architects have to search for ways of increasing the habitable, income-producing space without detracting from the building's character. At the basement level of the West Queen Anne School, floors have been raised and the outside ground level lowered so that occupants can walk through the French doors of their apartments directly into private gardens. Construction crews cut into the school's tall hip roofs to install additional windows, French doors, and small exterior decks in what had been the attic. Although these can be seen from the ground, they're positioned to avoid calling attention to themselves.

The same issue—how to turn unoccupied attic space into apartments without being conspicuous about it—arose at the Green Brier in Chicago. Tiny original windows along the perimeter of the Green Brier's attic would have let in too little light. Landmark Properties cut large holes in the flat roof, creating four top-floor atriums open to the sky, with windows and glass doors on most of the atriums' walls. Conse-

TOP AND RIGHT
Graham Gund's Church Court condominium complex in Boston, and the observatory at the top of its seven-story bell-tower apartment.
BELOW
The old Charlestown Navy Yard, now called Constitution Quarters and converted to housing.

quently, light penetrates the interiors of the new apartments on the uppermost floor, and the residents can sit in these new outdoor courtyards, sheltered from Chicago's winds.

Seattle abounds with imaginative solutions that could be used in conversion projects throughout the country. In the oldest section of downtown, Pioneer Square, additions have been built on the rooftops of old commercial and industrial buildings that have been converted to housing or to a combination of housing, retailing, and offices. Set back at least 10 feet from the roof's edge, these additions can be glimpsed from the street—they seem a kind of oasis in the sky—and yet the original profile of each building remains little disturbed. The new space increases the buildings' rentable square footage, and it offers self-employed people the prospect of two-level units, with their living area on one floor and their work on another. The roof decks are also a much-appreciated retreat from the busy streets below.

<hr>

Traditionally there have been three main approaches to preservation—restoration, rehabilitation, and renovation. Restoration entails returning a building to the character it had at some earlier period in its history—as the Boones did with their house in Springfield, Massachusetts. Rehabilitation implies that some concessions have been made to modern demands or economic pressures; much that's original is saved, but many compromises are struck. Renovation indicates a pronounced change in the building; the basic structure may survive, but with significant alterations.

Today many preservation projects don't fit neatly into any of these three categories. Often two or even all three of these approaches may be combined in a single building. The outside may get a pure restoration, while portions of the interior that are in good condition are rehabilitated and portions in disrepair are given a modern character. At Seattle's Fire Station 25, built in 1909, the local architectural firm of Stickney & Murphy retained most of the original exterior appearance while transforming the interior into sixteen apartments. The brick building had always drawn much of its charm from a succession of four segmental-arched bays, each with a door that opened to let horses pull their wagons to fires. The architects retained the arched openings, merely removing the old doors and substituting residential doors with windows above them. Where there had once been pavement in front of the four doors, Stickney & Murphy installed patios, each sitting behind a wrought iron fence. The firehouse, like most old schools, also had interiors that were tall enough to allow lofts to be placed in some of the units. Here, as in most other projects containing lofts, the bedroom loft is close to the core of the building, above a new kitchen and bathroom.

<hr>

Conversions are being carried out throughout the United States, but Massachusetts, which once based much of its economy on factories clustered next to sources of water power, contains some of the largest concentrations of nonresidential buildings turned into housing. In Lowell, a city that was once America's preeminent textile manufacturing center, old red brick mills have been converted to comfortable housing—usually subsidized apartments for elderly or low-income residents—and their exteriors have been kept intact except, in some notable instances, for the windows, which were considered too energy-inefficient or so bulky that elderly people would have difficulty opening and closing them. Inside, the ceilings in many of the buildings have been lowered to

188

reduce the volume of air that has to be heated and cooled. Some of the apartments feel new, yet the public areas of the building contain reminders of the building's age and its solidity. At Francis Gate, a turn-of-the-century shoe factory in Lowell that was redesigned by The Endeavor Group of Boston, wood posts and beams remain visible in the apartments and in public areas, their textures softened and warmed by sandblasting the old wood. At the base of a main stairway at Francis Gate, 3-foot-high boulders stand exposed. The massive door of what was once the factory's boiler is mounted on the wall of the social room.

A Boston architectural firm, Notter Finegold

Seattle's Fire Station 25 about 1920, and today with its driveways replaced by fenced patios.

& Alexander, took on a still more complicated challenge—converting the obsolete industrial structures of Boston's 130-acre Charlestown Navy Yard, which had been placed on the National Register of Historic Places after being decommissioned by the government in 1974. The architects began the huge undertaking by redesigning five large foundry and machine-shop buildings from the 1850s to the 1940s so that they could accommodate 367 apartments, called Constitution Quarters. The spine of the buildings, 60 feet high, became atriums—one of which stretches nearly 700 feet long in running through two of the buildings. Fabric mobiles now float in the spectacular atrium interiors. It is through the atriums, with their new floors of quarry tile and their trusswork painted a cheerful orange, that residents walk when entering or leaving their apartments.

To give the atriums a more comfortably residential scale, footbridges and glass elevators were built, in effect breaking the colossal interior into segments, and steps were added to connect the first-floor apartments to the atriums' street level, as if in an abstracted version of the half-flight of steps in front of nineteenth-century brownstones. Original monumental arches in the older buildings have been saved, their windows now belonging not to a mammoth industrial interior but to three stories of apartments. The historical and architectural integrity of the old buildings' exteriors remain largely intact even while the interiors, especially those of the apartments themselves, are strongly contemporary.

There are instances in which the authenticity of an exterior and the requirements for a comfortable interior come into conflict, and the comfort of the occupants is diminished. On the West Side of New York, at West 61st Street and Columbus Avenue, the Sofia warehouse underwent a metamorphosis in 1985–1986 that was both magnificent and disappointing. The twenty-six-story Sofia had been built in 1930 as one of New York's first vertical parking garages. Quite a few of the nation's early parking garages were strikingly handsome, and the Sofia must have ranked among the best. It had an exuberant Art Deco exterior, with vertical and horizontal bands enlivening the brickwork above an elaborately ornamental base. Later the Sofia became a storage warehouse.

By 1983 its increasingly desirable location, not far to the south of Lincoln Center, had become too valuable for a low-rent use like storage. The designated landmark's new owners, Aaron Green Companies and British Land of America, proposed to turn the first nine floors into office space and the rest into condominium apartments. The city's Landmarks Preservation Commission allowed the owners to insert 394 new windows into the Sofia's walls, which had been built with only a fraction of the number of openings that a residential or office structure would have had. The new casement windows, however, had to be set deeply into the openings to create a shadow effect that harmonized with the Art Deco character of the exterior, and their sizes had to match the patterns established by the original windows and ornamental banding.

Designers took some of the building's drawbacks and turned them into assets. The ceilings' heavy concrete beams—rudimentary structural elements that once were needed to support the weight of automobiles—were embellished by architects and decorators, in at least one in-

190

An industrial building in Boston's Charlestown Navy Yard at an early stage of conversion to apartments.

stance with gold leaf; instead of looking ponderous, the beams now give the ceilings a richly coffered effect. Some of the awkwardly placed pillars did a disappearing act. One way of accomplishing this involved placing a mirror in front of one face of the pillar and installing lighting in a recess between mirror and pillar; the combination of the reflection and the glow dematerialized the pillar. Bathrooms were surfaced with marble tiles and equipped with old-style cross-handle fixtures. The apartments have a sumptuous feeling—as they should, since some sold for more than $300 a square foot. But the disadvantage of restricting the windows to a size in keeping with the original openings and exterior banding was a loss of apparent spaciousness on the interior. Windows couldn't extend up to the ceiling; their widths were also constricted. More and bigger windows would have made the rooms feel more generous. In New York, an expansive view counteracts the effect of the small dimensions within. But at the Sofia, as at a large number of landmark projects across the nation, the requirement for preserving the public face of the building caused some sacrifice of livability within.

Some old buildings pose a question much different from that of the Sofia. When an old building is neither architecturally distinguished nor in a location that's in great demand, an architect may ask: why not alter the building drastically and give it a new image? This may be a building's only immediate hope for being turned around. One of the most dramatic examples of this approach stands on North Wells Street on the Near North Side of Chicago,

Completed atrium of the Navy Yard's Building 42 after construction of apartments along its perimeter.

across the street from the flashing lights of a pornographic bookstore. Chicago architect Kenneth Schroeder decided he had to generate a magnetic new image for a property he was trying to revive—a former Dr. Scholl's shoe-factory complex that had grown for nearly a century until it contained more than 30 buildings or additions.

Schroeder demolished some of the uninteresting recent structures in the interior of the two-block complex so that the apartments he created in the remaining buildings could be arranged around a pair of landscaped courtyards, secure against intruders and sheltered from the winds. The courtyards are oases of greenery and calm—valuable assets, since, as Schroeder puts it, "Chicago is a hard town. There's not much amenity in from the lake." The calm is not absolute, however. The architect installed glass and steel walkways on the upper levels facing the courtyards and painted the steel a dark red, infusing visual energy into buildings that otherwise would be mundane.

It was on the front that Schroeder made the most radical alteration. The part of the shoe factory that had faced North Wells Street was an ordinary brick building constructed in the 1960s —not much for an upwardly mobile white-collar Chicagoan to come home to. Schroeder believed that if the complex—in truth a motley assemblage—were to succeed, its new character would have to be announced unmistakably with some Postmodern razzle-dazzle, a cross between classicism and neon advertising. In the middle of the building facing North Wells, he knocked out a section 30 feet wide and inserted at its base a small limestone gatehouse—traditional in style, but not without its trendy touches. The name given to the complex, Cobbler Square, was written in neon tubing above its entrance. People will move into all sorts of

193

The Art Deco–style Sofia condominium after conversion from a storage warehouse, and one of the Sofia's apartments.

places if the buildings have style, and Cobbler Square, true to the sales techniques of the shoe industry, was destined to succeed at least partly on the basis of fashion.

The gatehouse sits under the forward edge of a three-story, skylighted courtyard leading to the apartments' lobby. This is a high-impact entrance, energetic enough to deflect a resident's attention away from the sleaziness across the street and to offset the prosaic character of the long corridors that wind through Cobbler Square's complicated interior. Schroeder also put imagination into the apartment designs. The 293 apartments, ranging from 450 to 1,450 square feet, contain more than 40 layouts, which suggests one of the redeeming virtues of converted buildings: individuality. Every unit is not stamped from the same pattern. There's room for idiosyncrasy and surprise. Some Cob-

bler Square apartments have artist-industrial-loft ambience, with exposed-brick interior walls, sandblasted wood joists, and ceilings 12–14 feet high. Some of the designs masterfully contrast the natural tones of old wood and brick against painted, exposed ductwork and against a sleek white kitchen and bathroom module (on top of which sits a small sleeping loft). It's a bracing, invigorating esthetic, unlike anything you'd ever find in a suburban cul-de-sac.

Reed ranch house outside of San Antonio.

Another preservationist approach involves using old buildings to help determine the character for new additions. About 35 miles northwest of San Antonio, on the rolling prairie below the Texas hill country, the architect Chris Carson had to make an appealing residence out of a house that had already undergone a considerable evolution. A cabin of cedar logs had been constructed in the 1850s, and a more substantial two-story limestone structure had been added to its front a few years later. The front portion was a version of a traditional "dog-trot" house, with an open corridor 10 feet wide running through its center to provide some relief from the heat in an era when the only air conditioning came from natural breezes blowing through. The walls were constructed of hand-chiseled limestone 14 inches thick. In the early 1980s, the house and its 200-acre ranch were purchased by Robert Reed, an oil-industry executive, and his wife, Maggie, who asked the architects to incorporate the two old portions of house into a design that would eventually include a sizable addition. The resulting house would have to offer modern comforts, yet retain its historic character.

Ford Powell & Carson turned the two first-floor rooms of the limestone house into a living room and a music room, and established two bedrooms upstairs beneath the cleaned and lightly sanded surfaces of the house's original wood ceilings. The architects placed the dining room in the log cabin and turned its low-ceilinged second floor into a children's playroom. To one side of the dining room, a new kitchen with a sink and counter of handmade tile was built in what had started out as a stone lean-to, and at the rear a laundry room and lavatory were added, faced in matching rough-cut limestone. Plans call for three more bedrooms to be eventually added to the rear, but even when all the additions are complete, what people will see as they drive down the country road and then down the ranch's long driveway will be the front of the old limestone house, sitting under a peaked metal roof much like those that became common after railroads began transporting tin to Texas in the late nineteenth century. The dog-trot has been enclosed now, but unobtrusively; the central hallway is shielded behind a set of traditional double doors that look as if they might have been the house's entrance for decades. To say that the house is handsome might be stretching things. Vernacular buildings often were not especially beautiful; some were downright homely. But the Reed house possesses a genuine and solid character, rooted in pioneer history, and that character has been valued and preserved in the latest stage of the house's evolution.

In Scottsdale, Arizona, the challenge that faced the Phoenix architectural firm of George Christensen & Associates was how to take a romantic but declining resort, the Casa Blanca, and add a series of compatible new buildings so that the 19-acre estate—originally a desert retreat that was now enveloped in suburban growth—could be turned into residential condominiums. Architect Robert Evans had designed the estate's original mansion in the 1930s for manufacturing heir Donald Kellogg. In the 1940s, George Borg of Borg-Warner purchased the property, later converting the mansion into an exclusive inn called the Casa Blanca and adding a new building topped by a stunning white Moroccan dome with diminutive domes accentuating its corners. In succeeding years, ownership changed several more times as the complex underwent what Christensen & Associates termed "adaptive abuse."

The architects restored the domed building as a single residence, one of its striking features being a magnificent ceiling with a quatrefoil opening that expands upward into the dome. The horseshoe-shaped mansion was turned into 35 townhouses averaging 1,280 square feet apiece. In stripping carpeting off the floors and removing an accumulation of unneeded partitions, the architects discovered long-forgotten tile floors, adobe fireplaces, and hand-hewn beams; these became focal points of the interiors, along with original doors, windows, and light fixtures. The architects restored the buildings' adobe walls, which have a magically strong yet soft quality when the clear Arizona light strikes their white surfaces. Equally important,

the landscape itself was renewed with arid-region vegetation and a more formal central garden, creating a setting that complemented the buildings' splendor.

Ninety-two new townhouses had to be added to the complex, but unlike architects, who, in the quest for originality, make new buildings look conspicuously different from old ones, Christensen & Associates designed the new buildings to blend in almost indistinguishably with the originals. Where the old buildings were constructed of adobe over a concrete frame, the new one- and two-story townhouses are built of cement block covered with stucco. Because attention was paid to unique features in the old buildings and to careful placement of the new units, Casa Blanca now contains condominiums with forty-five different floor plans.

At the base of Boston's Beacon Hill, Graham Gund Associates of Cambridge dealt with expansion on a much tinier scale. A one-story brick-enclosed structure had been converted from a garage into a two-room studio with garage and court. To this, the architectural firm added a second story with enough traditionalism to appear at home in an old city, yet with the traditional elements deployed in a playfully abstracted way. A trellis grid pops out from the surface of the new walls of cream-colored stucco—the effect is a kind of Modernist Tudor. The windows look like they're projecting from the trellis, as if they're not anchored to the wall at all. The gabled hip roof recalls the shapes of old houses without being literal about it. Inside, the 1,500-square-foot house appears light and spacious, in part because of the openness of the new second story. A minimum of barriers separates the kitchen, study, dining area, and living area. Above all these areas, a sloping ceiling expands the space upward. From a skylight and from glass in the gables, illumination pours

ABOVE

The cut-away and radically restyled entrance of Cobbler Square on Chicago's North Wells Street.

OPPOSITE

198 *The garage that Graham Gund expanded into a house in Boston's Beacon Hill, and a sectional view of its organization.*

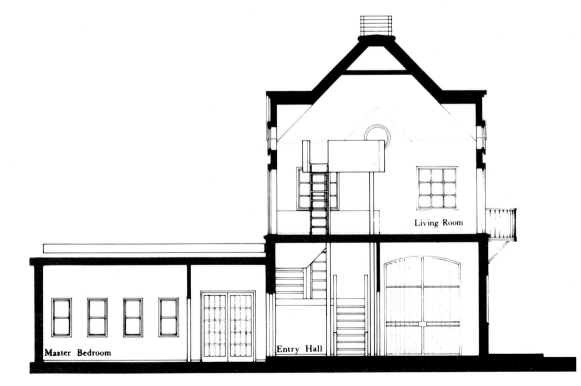

Living Room

Master Bedroom

Entry Hall

down onto oak trim, white gypsumboard walls, and quarry-tile floors.

━━━━

"A place without old buildings is like a person without a memory," wrote the British town planner Timothy Cantwell. Indeed, old buildings seem so essential that even a fire-ravaged remnant of historic construction can inspire the architectural imagination. One of Graham Gund's most rousing residential projects is Church Court, a condominium complex incorporating the ruins of an old church at Beacon Street and Massachusetts Avenue in Boston's Back Bay. At that intersection, a stone Richardsonian church was erected in 1891–1892, but after the Second World War the congregation dwindled and in 1971 the church was boarded up. Vandals attacked it, and in 1978 fire engulfed it.

Gund stepped in as both developer and architect, saving what he could—the corner tower, a portion of wall on Massachusetts Avenue, and the still-majestic Beacon Street façade, with its large rose window and its dignified series of three entrance arches. Gund inserted a few apartments into what remains of the original church structure, including one apartment that climbs, room by room, seven stories up the old tower. (Not surprisingly, this apartment was still for sale well after most of the other units had been occupied.)

Surviving walls near the streets help retain the visual character of the old church, but in addition, they provide edges for a landscaped courtyard where residents can sit. Rising to the rear are the walls of the new structure—a vibrant collection of reflective orange tile, dark and light granite, and red, brown, and buff brick, arranged in patterns that take some of their inspiration from Victorian buildings nearby. Angling, jutting, curving, pointing, this

new residential tower claims its place as a landmark on the portion of the church site that faces the Charles River. Yet it also relates well to the old church's remnants, receding into the background at Beacon and Massachusetts Avenue and letting the proud remains of the church dominate the intersection.

━━━━

There are other variants on preservation, too. In its broadest definition, preservation extends beyond major restoration, rehabilitation, and renovation. It includes modest additions, remodeling projects, and the continuing maintenance of older buildings. Many people have been choosing to add onto their homes rather than buy or build another house. At times, the addition can surpass the quality of the original house. This was the case in West Lake Hills, outside Austin, Texas, when Thomas and Carole Cable decided to expand a 1960s house whose most pleasing feature was its large, wooded lot. The Cables—he is an English professor, she a fine arts librarian—needed an addition that would serve as a home library and office.

How do you build a distinguished addition onto an undistinguished house? One way is to leave some distance between the old and the new. Austin architect Lawrence W. Speck designed an octagonal structure that stands about 20 feet from the house. Connecting the two is a corridor with a stone floor, with windows on one side, and with a solid wall on which part of the Cables' collection of seventeenth- and eighteenth-century ink-and-wash drawings is displayed. The 35-foot-high octagon is placed so that it, rather than the original house, domi-

An interior at Church Court in Boston, where floor plans vary widely.

The almost free-standing octagonal library addition of the Cable house in West Lake Hills, Texas, by Lawrence W. Speck Associates, and its two-story interior.

nates the view from the driveway and the road. One of the pleasing characteristics of old buildings in the Texas hill country is their use of native limestone, and the exterior of the study is formed of limestone blocks with a rugged-looking split face. Furthermore, the structure is topped by a cupola with windows on all eight sides that let light in and heat out; in summer, the breezes keep the library 10 degrees cooler than the main house. Stone that was found on the site frames the library's fireplace, and oak gives a natural tone to the floor. Structural support on the interior comes from eight columns covered with pine boards, with quarter-round molding where they join. The columns thus look pleasingly detailed, but without requiring a difficult or expensive level of craftsmanship.

In many houses, what's needed is primarily rearrangement of the existing interior. The architectural firm Centerbrook in Essex, Connecticut, was commissioned to redesign part of a classic New England farmhouse that had been owned by the same family since 1746. Like many old rural houses, this one had grown over the years, a long "ell" extending back from the main 2½-story portion and then another small ell branching off from that. The new occupants didn't really need more room; what they wanted was a spacious eat-in kitchen—which could be inserted into the first ell—and a laundry and potting shed.

Architect J. P. Chadwick Floyd, with architect Stephen L. Lloyd as project manager, ended up demolishing some of the most recent extension and putting a flagstone patio where it had stood. To tie together interior and exterior, the architects placed a white-painted post-and-beam structure over the patio and extended it to the older ell, where it serves as the structural system. Skylights in the roof of this ell illuminate a massive new fireplace chimney made of granite

cobblestones—or, to be more accurate, the chimney actually extends up *through* the skylight area, giving the room a dramatic focal point and at the same time absorbing solar heat to help keep the room warm.

Heat-absorbing floors of black slate complement the passive-solar design. Some of the sunlight enters through windows that recall architecture from years ago—sidelights and segmental-arched windows surrounding a set of French doors, with simple barn sash inserted below the eaves. The barn sash is ingenious because it's been placed together in an unconventional way—seven of these horizontally proportioned fixed-glass windows lined up side by side. The result is a remodeling that reveals twentieth-century imagination and at the same time reaffirms the character of an eighteenth-century dwelling.

In the expensive housing market of Santa Monica, California, Buzz Yudell of Moore Ruble Yudell had to find shelter that, as a young architect, he could afford. He discovered a slapped-together 1940s bungalow and redid the entire building, changing almost everything. Where the front wall once had two badly mismatched windows and a humble-looking doorway, Yudell did some rearranging and installed a well-crafted grouping—door, sidelights, and windows—with delicately proportioned muntins, reminiscent of designs from sixty or so years ago. A series of four curved concentric steps radiating from the doorway makes the entrance ensemble even more inviting.

The four arcs outside the doorway set the stage for a more powerful curve within. Where the house once had a half-dozen boxy little rooms, its main sitting area is now an almost-complete ellipse. Large cutouts in the curving walls introduce alcoves for seating, dining, sleeping, and library areas. These subsidiary

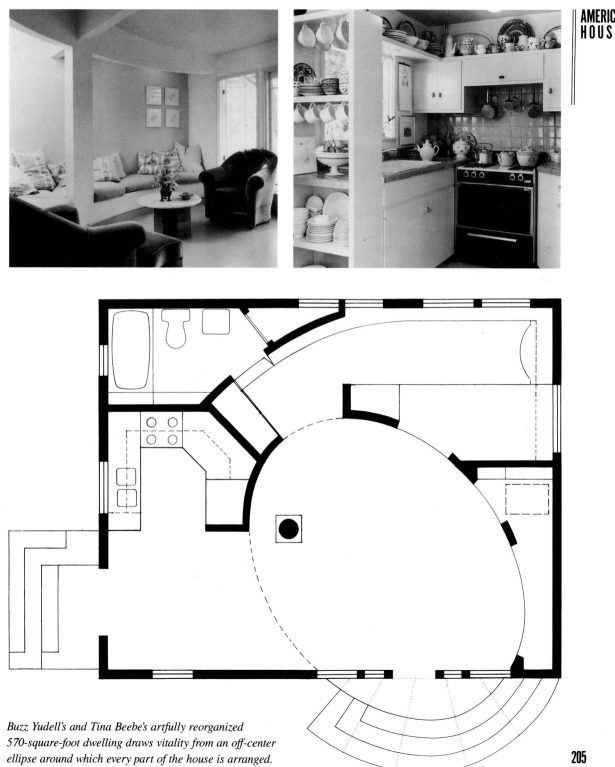

*Buzz Yudell's and Tina Beebe's artfully reorganized
570-square-foot dwelling draws vitality from an off-center
ellipse around which every part of the house is arranged.*

areas thus present themselves as distinct and well-defined parts of the house while at the same time contributing a needed sense of depth to the main sitting area. The bungalow is tiny—a mere 570 square feet—but its elliptical shape and walls with openings convey a sense that there is more room slightly hidden from view. (In fact, one room that's entirely hidden away is the bathroom; its door is cleverly concealed as a section of bookshelves in the library.) Throughout the bungalow, Yudell's wife, color consultant Tina Beebe, used a luminous gray floor that reflects the light and helps the interior feel larger. The whole transformation was accomplished for less than $10,000.

From Brooklyn, then, to Santa Monica, from four-story brownstones to former factories to 1940s bungalows, the examples of interesting uses of old (or not-quite-old) buildings are innumerable. In a relatively few years, methods of handling older buildings have grown markedly more varied and more sophisticated. Important advances have taken place in materials and in thinking about how to infuse life and utility into buildings that would once have been deemed obsolete. For those who admire old buildings, this is a hopeful time. The three Rs—restoration, rehabilitation, and renovation—have all entered the mainstream of American housing, and they promise to remain major influences for the foreseeable future.

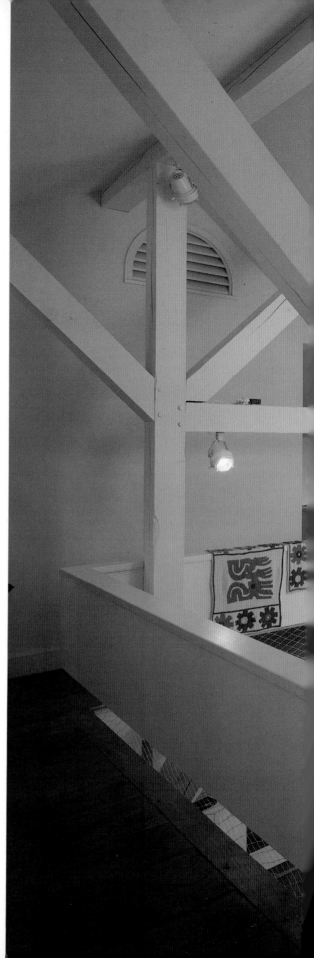

Granite cobblestone chimney and white-painted post-and-beam structure in a Connecticut farmhouse kitchen redesigned by J. P. Chadwick Floyd.

Chapter Six

The Quest for Richness

An archetypal house shape frames an Atlantic view while also defining the patio edge for a house by Graham Gund Associates.

For most of us, a house is the one form of architecture that we can imbue with our own, highly personal sense of beauty and utility. It's the one design enterprise over which we exercise a heartening measure of control. Few of us have a hand in fashioning the monumental public structures of our age, but the house, with its far more intimate and malleable scale, offers ample possibilities for involvement. A home can amount to much more than shelter—it can be a powerfully emotive building, one that reflects in lasting, three-dimensional form the feelings and aspirations of its owner. With intelligence and care, a house and its grounds can mature into a habitat embodying individualized taste and judgment, ideas and emotions ranging all the way from the whimsical to the profound.

It is this expressive capacity that sets many of today's houses strikingly apart from houses of the recent past. Beginning with the construction boom following the Second World War and for roughly three decades thereafter, there was a strong emphasis in the United States on erecting houses as fast as they could be put up; whether the houses possessed any depth of feeling was a question builders didn't worry about much. Although builder houses sometimes exhibited a few stylistic flourishes, their predominant quality was simplicity. They were best described as neutral; function was valued more than character. The split-level and the raised ranch, to mention two of the most popular designs of the 1960s and 1970s, may have organized their interior space economically and conveniently, but did they provoke delight? Not usually. That's where today's houses are trying to do better: they are trying to connect with feelings and ambitions, not just to

Entrance to the Hal Box house, Austin, Texas.

Sometimes a view is enhanced by the simplest of frames.

provide a bland package of utility, economy, and convenience.

Indeed, one of the notable developments of the past decade has been that, even though the price of housing has skyrocketed, Americans have for the most part rejected the idea of going "back to basics," back to simplified, Spartan little houses, in an effort to cut costs. Rather than settle for a slightly less expensive house that lacks emotion and importance, homebuyers instead demand a residence that projects a sense of fullness and lives up to its lofty price tag. They ask that the house offer touches that are special. Increasingly, the house is expected to possess some dignity and romance.

In 1986, *Builder,* the official magazine of the American homebuilding industry, published an article encouraging builders to incorporate 211

The Sterrett house near San Diego reveals its organization only gradually.

In the past several years, the architecture of the great sixteenth-century Italian classicist Andrea Palladio has attracted a new wave of admiration, and today the Palladian-inspired round-arched window—often abstracted, but with its ancestry still recognizable—lends a measure of grandeur to hundreds of thousands of new homes. Generally, houses are assuming more active, intricate profiles. A growing complexity has shown up in the walls, windows, and roof lines of expensive and inexpensive houses alike throughout the country. More and more rarely do the walls of houses run from end to end in a straight line, beneath a plain roof of uninterrupted and unembellished pitch. Some of the new intricacy is cloyingly overdone, and there will inevitably be a move away from such excesses. But on the whole, richer-feeling houses appear to be with us for the foreseeable future, their place secured by a burgeoning interest in visually and emotionally satisfying features.

such elements as projecting window areas—bays, bows, or boxier, more squared-off window extensions—into the kitchens, living rooms, and master bedrooms of houses then in the planning stage. *Builder* praised these protruding windows for letting in plenty of light and for making it easier for parents to watch their children, but the main purpose of such features goes beyond either of those functions; the primary objective, in the words of William J. Devereaux of Berkus Group Architects, is "to create more interesting space inside the house and provide some animation on the outside. On the exterior we want to create a sense of detail." The increasing attention focused on alluring windows is just one example of the widespread desire for houses that convey a sense of depth and completeness. Increasingly, American houses

212 reflect a national quest for richness.

A spectacular example of this quest for richness is a house that local architect Rob Wellington Quigley designed for a corner property in the Fairbanks Ranch, a luxurious development in the rolling hills north of San Diego, where the actor Douglas Fairbanks once had a fishing and hunting retreat. Quigley's clients, James K. Sterrett II and Nyda Jopling Sterrett, began the design process by putting down on paper the qualities they were looking for in a house. "Each room, each view, and each passage should spark curiosity and encourage one to try and discover what lies beyond it," the Sterretts wrote. "There

Palms and low plantings complement the house's simple, powerful forms. Elevation drawings show northwest façade (top) *and courtyard façade* (bottom).

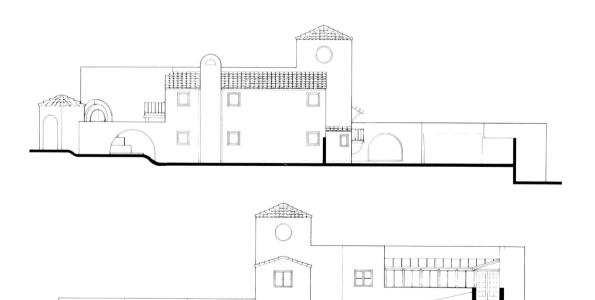

is no need to assault a viewer's eyes," they went on, "but the house should command attention." A strong presence is something that many Americans, especially those with plentiful financial resources, would like to have in a home, but the Sterretts had a complication to overcome: they were going to build a house of about 2,400 square feet in a lavish development where the neighboring houses were often three times that size.

Quigley's solution was a house that appears much larger than it actually is. Along the two streets that the house faces, the architect stretched out the exterior, making the house relatively thin—about one room deep—but substantially longer than it would otherwise have been. The walls facing the streets gain a still more imposing presence from the fact that their continuous beige stucco surfaces are interrupted by windows only to a limited extent; most of the street-side windows are relatively small. The great majority of the Sterretts' windows instead look out on a private courtyard in the house's center.

Facing one of the streets, a low wall extends outward, enclosing portions of the landscape and enhancing the property's sense of depth, tying house and grounds together while also establishing a horizontal base behind which the house can rise up. One of the things that makes the house's long walls powerfully romantic is their shape; they form an elaborate composition that is anchored at its western end by a massive, tile-roofed square tower and at its most prominent corner by a colossal entrance rotunda. The façade trails off toward the northeast with a picturesque wall reminiscent of old adobe ruins that have melted away in the rain.

The grand culmination of the Sterrett house's courtyard. Symmetry reinforces the effect.

The interplay of shapes—a massive round-topped chimney joins these other elements in punctuating the exterior—is complex enough that Quigley was able to keep the surfaces themselves extremely simple, thus avoiding large outlays for expensive craftsmanship. The forceful, simple stucco shapes also gain a great deal of charm from their contrast to the lush landscape. Architecture by itself is almost never sufficient: low plants at the base of the walls and tall palm trees rising above compensate for any lack of softness in the walls themselves. Here, under the clear, benevolent California light, a charming marriage of building and grounds has been brought into being.

Inside, Quigley gave the house an atmosphere that's both Mediterranean and modern. The interior focuses on the courtyard, as is true of houses in many regions with a warm, dry climate. In the center of the tiled courtyard is a garden, and at one corner—leading down to a second plaza containing a swimming pool and spa—is a double staircase, the kind of architectural device that establishes a classical sense of balance and elegance. But instead of placing heavy wrought iron along the edges of balconies, as Mediterranean antecedents would have suggested, Quigley chose curving pipe rail. Columns supporting the balconies are unembellished cylinders, more contemporary than traditional. What Quigley did was not so much revive the past as reinterpret it in contemporary terms for clients who told him that, while they like Moorish architecture, they also enjoy the flowing, open spaces of modern art galleries. There is a lively balance between symmetry and variation, between serenity and vigor. Just as the Sterretts had hoped, there are enough surprises to make a visitor want to keep exploring.

Quigley once offhandedly described the Sterrett house as "a little schmaltzy," perhaps be-

The romantic courtyard path to the Pylman residence in Chandler, Arizona, by George W. Christensen.

cause of features like the entry rotunda with its double set of curving stairs or because of the generally romantic flavor that pervades the entire house. A tinge of defensiveness shouldn't be surprising to anyone familiar with the strictures of Modernism in architecture. Modernists looked for form to be generated by function, for the building to reveal how it was constructed, for walls to express the volume they contained —for approaches to design that were much less at ease with historical custom and sentiment than the Sterrett house shows itself to be. Stern Modernist dogma continues to exert a lingering influence over architects, making many of them anxious about developing romantic designs that use history as a starting point. Nevertheless, the encouraging trend, gathering force rapidly

in recent years, is for architects to become receptive to history and to acknowledge the importance of the images of home that people carry in their heads. Quigley says, for instance, that he is "interested in reinterpreting the idea of the Arcadian dream in southern California" —which often means finding a way to design houses that are somehow rooted in the architectural heritage of California's early Spanish missions.

Across the Sunbelt, there has been a strikingly widespread revival of elements of the Spanish building tradition. With varying degrees of authenticity or abstraction, a Spanish or a more generally Mediterranean heritage is influencing hundreds of thousands of new houses—espe-

cially in California, Arizona, and Florida—that are being constructed not only by merchant homebuilders but also by some of the region's leading architects. In Phoenix, for instance, George W. Christensen, who studied under Mies van der Rohe at the Illinois Institute of Technology, designs some of his clients' houses in Spanish or other styles with a strongly historical character and emphasizes that—contrary to what the strict Modernists would have had us believe—"it's serious work." He often takes pains to give exterior walls a smooth white plaster finish, more historically accurate than the rough texture accepted by most homebuilders, and he thickens the walls surrounding windows and doors to a depth of 12–24 inches for a sense of solidity. (If a wall contains no windows, he may design it 7 inches thick. In walls that are interspersed with windows, additional stud framing underneath the stuccoed surface increases the thickness, so that windows can have deep sills on both their interior and exterior sides.) Christensen also employs well-

ABOVE
The entrance to a house by Howard Barnstone in Houston's Indian Circle.
OPPOSITE
View of the courtyard. The house's organization is indicated in the drawing.

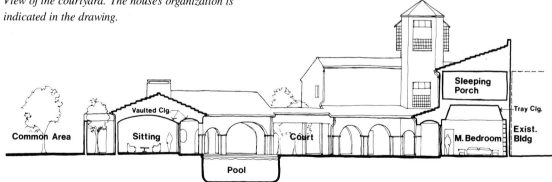

*View through the dining room to the courtyard in
Barnstone's Indian Circle residence.*
OVERLEAF
The open-air shower off the master bedroom (left), *and
the living room, which on one side looks out to the
courtyard* (right).

220

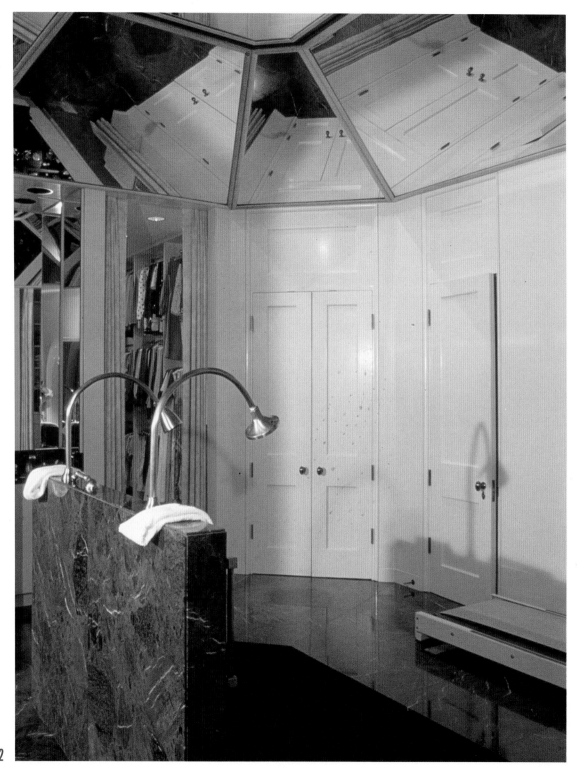

crafted traditional elements such as quatrefoil windows and tiled walkways.

Like any discerning architect, Christensen avoids styles ill-suited to the locale—no Tudor in the desert—and he likes having the latitude to reinterpret history rather than reproduce it literally, as in a period house. Out-and-out copying of the past appeals to few, if any, talented architects. The salient fact, however, is that both among designers brought up during the heyday of Modernism and among architects educated during the fifteen or twenty years since, history and tradition are exerting an increasingly strong attraction.

In Houston, architect Howard Barnstone won a reputation in the 1950s for designing crisp, disciplined Modernist houses—elegant residences with walls of glass and relatively cool, abstract forms. But he began to break with the Miesian esthetic in the mid-1960s, and the change of attitude became more pronounced as Barnstone immersed himself in studying the work of John F. Staub, architect of some of Houston's finest eclectic houses dating back to the 1920s. The Barnstone who made a name working in the minimalist idiom of Mies now feels comfortable designing historically inspired residences. His Peterkin house in the Indian Circle subdivision of Houston, designed with the assistance of associate architect Edward Rogers, exemplifies a quest for richness through historical imagery and through fine materials and craftsmanship.

One writer described the Peterkin house as "reminiscent of a country home in Spain, reflecting Northern Italianate influence." Barnstone himself describes it simply as Tuscan. Like houses in rural Tuscany, the Peterkin home turns away from its surroundings—a collection of townhouses sitting protected behind the exclusive subdivision's guarded metal gates. Its exterior walls are plain, its outward-looking

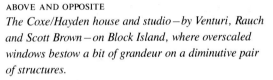

ABOVE AND OPPOSITE
The Coxe/Hayden house and studio—by Venturi, Rauch and Scott Brown—on Block Island, where overscaled windows bestow a bit of grandeur on a diminutive pair of structures.

windows few. In the Mediterranean manner, this house reserves its delights for those who have been invited in—and then reveals a spectacular oasis at its center. Visible straight ahead from the entry is a courtyard—large, irregularly shaped, and adorned with palm trees and flowering plants. On one side of the courtyard are a swimming pool and sitting areas, some sunny, some shaded. On the other, secluded behind a wall of flat rocks and flowering plants, is a patio adjoining the master bedroom suite.

In a direct line of sight from the entrance is the courtyard's centerpiece—a freestanding, classically inspired arch that echoes an arcade surrounding the courtyard. This grand arch, spanning a limestone walkway, accentuates the courtyard's air of dignity. Whereas the arcade is plain-surfaced, the arch is boldly ornamented with projecting bands and a prominent keystone. The series of arches around the courtyard's perimeter establishes a stately rhythm, and the freestanding arch in the center brings the rhythm to a grand culmination.

*Riverplace, a waterfront redevelopment project by Zane Yost & Associates along the Quinnipiac River in New Haven,
Connecticut, uses variations on the Victorian Stick Style and an abundance of protruding porches and decks to
magnify its appeal and fit into a historic neighborhood.*

227

Behind the arcade, most of the house's rooms have glass walls, displaying refreshing views of the courtyard garden. One of those rooms is an elegant combination of kitchen and family area, where, under an oak-surfaced ceiling, the family can prepare informal meals. This is only one of several places for cooking. Nearby is a larger kitchen in which the household staff work. One flight down is a small kitchen that can serve guests in an adjoining concrete-vaulted wine cellar. Even the master bedroom suite contains its own small kitchen, so the owners can make breakfast or get a snack without venturing into the rest of the house.

Throughout the Peterkin house, surfaces have been crafted of fine materials—African granite on walls in the butler's pantry, mahogany double doors in the formal living room, smooth round limestone columns set between large sheets of window glass in the dining room. The dining-room ceiling is coffered and decorated with stenciling by a New Mexico artist. Probably the most fanciful element of the house is an eight-sided tower that ascends from a rear corner and offers balcony views down into the courtyard, across the house's series of barrel-tile roofs, and out into the neighborhood.

Of all the styles being revived today, Spanish is the most prolific; it seems to fit a warm climate, and more houses are being built in the Sunbelt than anywhere else. But throughout the country, other styles that evoke the past are also on the ascendancy. Bursts of Art Deco–inspired styling have appeared in southern Florida. In the Northeast, a number of architects, including Robert A. M. Stern of New York City, have been reinterpreting the Shingle style of the late nineteenth century, one of the finest modes of residential architecture ever to appear on the American scene. Victorian design, predominantly vertical and often heavily ornamented, has experienced a nationwide upsurge after decades of being regarded as the epitome of bad taste. Perhaps most striking of all, there has even been a minor return to classicism, led by architect Allan Greenberg of New Haven. For decades, classical buildings were considered beyond the pale; few architects had any interest in designing them, and those that did manage to get built failed to win attention from the architectural press. So it's a sign of an extraordinary shift in architectural sensibilities that an architect like Greenberg is designing in a genuinely classical manner and being respectfully treated by the architectural establishment. A classical house designed by Greenberg and based on George Washington's Mount Vernon has not only attracted serious attention but was chosen by *Architectural Record* in 1986 as one of its "Houses of the Year."

Each of these styles bestows its own kind of richness—the richness of history, memory, and association. Houses that recall the past are able to tap into a reservoir of understanding and affection, stirring emotions that more uncompromisingly modern designs are often unable to arouse. That historical styles are being used by major architects and market-oriented builders alike is more than a coincidence; it is cause for celebration, for it means that builders—who in the past have often botched the job of producing traditional houses—may be able to learn from unusually talented designers about how to use historical elements and atmosphere knowledgeably and imaginatively. No longer are "serious" architects living, for the most part, in an entirely different world from builders.

It goes without saying that a house modeled on Mount Vernon or a lavish house like the Peterkins' is more likely to achieve a sense of richness than are houses built on more modest budgets. But that truism can be taken only so far. The fact is, a great many homes of people who are not wealthy are also finding ways to establish a measure of sumptuousness and importance. Some major homebuilders are shifting to more and larger moldings and trim to dignify and dress up their houses. Some are using hardwood floors rather than the usual wall-to-wall carpeting over plywood to establish some warmth and character. Many two-story houses are incorporating double-height foyers with beautiful carved wood entry doors. (An alternative to consider is designing the entrance on a comfortable, more modest scale and saving the dramatic effect—such as a magnificent view—until after the foyer. The delay and surprise can make a special feature all the more breathtaking.) Some designers divide living rooms from dining rooms by installing handsome half-columns on low wooden partitions, or they achieve the same purpose with full columns,

which are not necessarily expensive; they're stock building components, readily available.

Even some recently built subsidized housing boasts features that invest it with dignity and importance. In projects as far removed from each other as forty-three-unit-per-acre Somerset Parkside apartments in Sacramento, California (designed by Van der Ryn, Calthorpe & Partners of Inverness, California), and Empire Townhouses, eighteen townhouses designed by Weese Hickey Weese Architects of Chicago for the tiny town of Empire, Michigan, subsidized housing has moved toward emphasizing the individuality of each household. Instead of the

BELOW AND OVERLEAF
The familiar shapes of older rural and small-town houses were reworked by Weese Hickey Weese to give the Empire Townhouses in Michigan a charm usually lacking in developments sponsored by the Farmers Home Administration.

institutional look that long plagued government-aided housing, the apartments in Sacramento have varying roof lines, as well as gateways, balconies, decks, and even some private yards, to enhance the character and livability of the development. In Empire, the look of the townhouses is unpretentious and nostalgic, modeled on the pleasant, familiar appearance of older rural and small-town wooden houses. Rather than resembling a one-story motel, with flat roofs and parking right in front—as has been the fate of many small-town subsidized developments—Empire Townhouses uses steep roofs, gables, and front porches to give each unit more presence and individuality.

The desire for a proud appearance as well as for safety has led to a proliferation of gates in residential complexes—some of them manned by a security force, some equipped with gates that respond to a code or a card, some mainly symbolic. These are not unprecedented elements in American residential developments. Theodore Dreiser observed in 1915 that in upper-class Midwestern neighborhoods it was becoming increasingly common to find "a street with a great gate at either end." Those gates, open and unguarded, provoked conflicting impulses in Dreiser. He scoffed at them as "pretentious," but ultimately had to admit that these gated streets were "quite impressive." The troublesome issue today is that many of the gates in new developments are not simply symbolic structures, imposing but open; they are all-too-genuine barriers, excluding the great majority of nonresidents. American society depends on a confidently democratic sentiment, and the danger is that these guarded gates will foster a

breakdown of valuable trust and good will, especially as it becomes increasingly apparent that neighborhoods of above-average means are shutting themselves off from those with less money. Unless this trend is reversed, a price will likely be paid one day for taking the desire for exclusivity (and safety) to such an extreme.

Fortunately, many houses are sending a different message by adopting features that suggest friendliness. In the past few years, the front porch in particular has made a surprising comeback. No other architectural element summons up so much promise of sociability and gregariousness as a front porch. In the Gulf Coast resort town of Seaside, in the Florida Panhandle, new houses are required to have front porches, and the porches must be big enough—usually at least half as wide as the house and at least 8 feet deep—and close enough to the street—usually 16 feet—that they're likely to be used and likely to spark conversations between residents and pedestrians. "We want to make the streets and the houses fronting the streets more friendly," explains Robert S. Davis, Seaside's developer.

"We're attempting to build a town made up of neighborhoods," says Davis, who prepared himself for the project by traveling through the small older towns of the Southeast, observing what made those communities successful, both visually and socially. At Seaside, Davis put into effect a town plan that tightly defined the design of the streets, grounds, and houses. The houses had to evoke an old-time flavor. Often they have painted latticework at their bases. Cupolas and widow's walks rise above some of the houses' ribbed metal roofs. Windows are predominantly vertical, like those in nineteenth-century

The pergola at left joins in a system of garden architecture that gives a strong sense of identity to the Rosewalk area of Seaside, Florida.

OVERLEAF
Aerial view of the Rosewalk area, where Orr & Taylor designed houses with towers, porches, and widows' walks looking onto the common gardens.

Main entry gate to Rosewalk.

houses, and tall double-hung windows set into clapboard walls predominate.

Seaside's is an open, homey, small-town kind of architecture, and its appeal goes deeper than appearance. The streets are narrow and paved with brick so that people will feel comfortable going for walks. Lining the front yards is picket fence that Davis says "gives a soft definition to the public and private realms and makes the street feel smaller and more human in scale."

The emphasis on investing houses and communities with more feeling and character is not yet standard in the American homebuilding industry. Some builders have a long way to go.

Behind the gate is Orr & Taylor's "veranda classic" house, whose living and dining areas are on the second floor for views and breezes.
OVERLEAF
Bristling as if with antennae, the home of architect Bart Prince hovers above its modest lot in Albuquerque.

236

The Hanna studio, an addition by Bart Prince to an adobe-style house in Albuquerque. Much of the exterior is faced in ceramic tile and translucent plastic.

240 *A study in Prince's own house. Semi-circular door pivots open to a deck.*

But attentiveness to the features that make houses more satisfying is clearly on the rise. Indeed, one of the things that's remarkable about many recent American houses is their ability to concentrate on achieving the sense of dignity or individuality or traditionalism that their inhabitants want and yet to adapt at the same time to technological and sociological changes. New synthetic materials may be used, stringent energy-conservation methods may be adopted, nontraditional households may be accommodated, and yet those changes remain largely invisible in the shape and appearance of the house.

There have been times in the past when architects argued that the nature of the American house would have to undergo some fundamental alteration, reflecting different ways of building or reflecting departures from the "standard" family. But the freedom we enjoy in shaping our houses has turned out to be much greater than anticipated. To a large extent, the house can be whatever we want it to be. It can adjust to contemporary conditions very quietly, if, as is often the case, that's what people prefer. It can offer the reassurance of tradition and embody the memories of the past, as many houses are now doing.

It can also explore bold new directions. Scattered mostly across the western half of the nation, for instance, are a few architects who design houses of astonishingly original form, houses for which general trends are irrelevant. The work of these architects—sometimes described as "organic," sometimes classified as the "American School," since it has little to do with the International Style or with European antecedents—will never be the American mainstream, and yet it remains important, if only to demonstrate the wondrous directions that unfet-

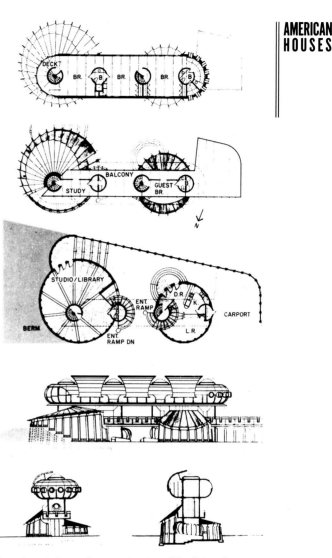

Drawings indicate the organization of the Prince house.
OVERLEAF
Top of a spiral staircase, where radiating rails are formed of steel reinforcing bars. Sunlight enters through a plastic dome.

tered creativity can take. Among these architects is Albuquerque's Bart Prince, who, like several of the others, worked for the late Oklahoma architect Bruce Goff, one of the most individualistic and idiosyncratic American designers of the twentieth century. Prince has 241

Softly carpeted spiraling stairs in the Prince house.

Prince's work studio receives generous natural light through ribbed plastic translucent insulating panels.

243

produced buildings so extraordinary that people call them by names like "the silo house," "the snail house," and "the spaceship."

Prince's own house suggests a cross between a spaceship and a large caterpillar or centipede. Located on a narrow corner lot in a quiet neighborhood, the house rises three stories, and the top level is like that of no other house in Albuquerque—or anywhere else, for that matter. Prince said he wanted the bedrooms as high as possible—up where there are vistas of the Sandia Mountains and more privacy—and he wanted this top level to have a sculptural shape that would be stable in Albuquerque's sometimes strong winds. Consequently the 90-foot-long, 24-foot-wide third level is a continuous curve—some of it covered with tongue-and-groove fir and spruce, but much of it fitted with rounded Plexiglas panels—that affords commanding views out and lets the sun in. Every 4 feet or so along the southern exposure, a 5-foot-high fiberglass tube full of water catches the sun and stores some warmth for overnight. The tubes rise out of a continuous wall seat, covered with carpeting that climbs halfway up the curved walls. "I wanted to have the floors flow into the walls," Prince explained, "and I wanted it basically to be a soft area, where you can sit on the floor and lean back against the wall to read or whatever."

Spiky 8-foot-long black pipes hold a long solar screen above the windows, blocking unwanted heat gain in the summer. At one curving end of the house, metal supports poke outward in various directions, some of them for use as handholds when Prince goes up on the roof. They look like antennae of a gigantic insect. Below the top floor, there's an outdoor deck—a necessary amenity, Prince felt, on a lot only 45–60 feet wide. Two great round areas covered with ceramic tile on their exterior contain most of the living and working areas on the two lower floors.

This fantastic combination of circles, spheres, and spirals may be descended from some of the geometry of Frank Lloyd Wright, whom Prince studied intensively during his student days. Prince himself said matter-of-factly, "I'm interested in using whatever form does the job, fulfills the design solution, at the moment." Prince insists on freedom from architectural preconceptions, and he ignores national trends. The result, in this case, is a clunky, weird, wonderful, and invigorating building—not a model for American housing but a testament to the importance of believing in your own ideas. As Prince himself has said, "Imagination is the key."

And that is a key to today's American houses in general—to their wide-reaching diversity, their array of responses to the questions of how people choose to live, how people capitalize on a setting, how they make the most of the climate, how they turn ideas into physical form. This is a period of abundant choices, a time when the nature of the house frequently varies —and should vary still more—in accordance with personal needs and tastes. Many house designers, as we have seen, are invoking history. Many are striving for drama, for presence and personality. But the essential ingredient— the fundamental requirement of homes that are satisfying—is imagination, for the range of possibilities open today is vaster than it has ever been.

OPPOSITE
Prince's addition to the Seymour house in Los Altos, California, lets the occupants feel as if they're suspended amid the branches of oak trees.
OVERLEAF
Prince's family-area addition to the top of the Worley house in Albuquerque.

244

Sources

The information in this book came from many sources—most notably, hundreds of visits to houses and housing developments throughout the United States and interviews with people involved in nearly every aspect of residential design and construction. In addition, the nation's architectural, building, and planning journals greatly enhanced my understanding. The literature on American housing is vast, and there is no need to review all of the publications that ultimately influenced this book. Some books, however, contributed so directly and strongly to *American Houses* that they should be acknowledged by name. David P. Handlin's *The American Home: Architecture and Society—1815–1915* (Little, Brown, 1979) is a valuable history from which I have drawn some of my description (in Chapter One) of attitudes toward the domestic landscape. *The Place of Houses,* by Charles Moore, Gerald Allen, and Donlyn Lyndon (Holt, Rinehart & Winston, 1979) provides an especially thoughtful examination of the varying ways in which houses respond to their settings. My presentation of the history of American attitudes toward the layout of suburbs comes from several sources, the most significant being John Reps, *The Making of Urban America: A History of City Planning in the United States* (Princeton University Press, 1965), Norman T. Newton, *Design on the Land: The Development of Land-*scape Architecture (Belknap Press, 1971), and Robert A. M. Stern, *Pride of Place: Building the American Dream* (Houghton-Mifflin, 1986). Barrie B. Greenbie gives a succinct explanation of how buildings create a pleasant sense of enclosure of outdoor space on page 41 of his *Spaces: Dimensions of the Human Landscape* (Yale University Press, 1981). Readers who want to learn more about the environmental ideas incorporated into the Village Homes development in Davis, California, should turn to Michael Corbett's *A Better Place to Live: New Designs for Tomorrow's Communities* (Rodale Press, 1981).

A trustworthy guide to superinsulation, which contributed to Chapter Three, is *The Superinsulated Home Book,* by J. D. Ned Nisson and Gautum Dutt (Wiley, 1985). Ralph Knowles's calculations on designing housing to receive solar heat, referred to in Chapter Three, can be found in his book, *Sun Rhythm Form* (MIT Press, 1981). Readers interested in timber-frame construction (Chapter Four) should consult *Building the Timber Frame House,* by Tedd Benson with James Gruber (Scribner's, 1980). My discussion of house additions in Chapter Five owes a debt to Duo Dickinson, *Adding On: An Artful Guide to Affordable Residential Additions* (McGraw-Hill, 1985).

Photo Credits

Pages 134-135: © Nicholas King.
138, 139 (all): cour. Arco Building Products.
141: cour. Anozira Development, Inc.
142-143: © 1987 Philip Langdon.
146-147: © 1987 Philip Langdon.
150, 151 (top): cour. Cardinal Industries, Inc.; **(bottom):** © 1987 Philip Langdon.
153: cour. Cardinal Industries, Inc.
154-155: Richard Mandelkorn, © 1986 Timberpeg (architect: Lyman S. A. Perry).
155 (top): cour. Yankee Barn Homes; **(bottom):** Joseph St. Pierre, cour. Maine Post & Beam Co., Inc.
156: Richard Mandelkorn, © 1986 Timberpeg (architect: Lyman S. A. Perry).
158 (all): Tafi Brown, cour. Benson Woodworking Company.
159: Sandy Agrafiotis, cour. Maine Post & Beam Co., Inc.
160-161, 161 (both): © 1985 Nicholas King.
162 (all), 163: © 1985 Jeffrey Westman.
167: Signy Spiegel, cour. Kaleidoscope Designs.
169: Jeff Heatley, cour. Norman Jaffe, A.I.A.
171 (both): Steve Rosenthal, cour. Graham Gund Architects.
173, 174 (all), 175, 176-177: © Michael Gordon.
180: Les Boschke, cour. Landmark Properties, Inc.
181: Tom Yanul, cour. Landmark Properties, Inc.
183: cour. Historic Landmarks for Living.
184 (top): Leslie Tonkin, cour. Tonkin/Koch Architects, Inc.; **(bottom):** Richard Cardwell, cour. Cardwell/Thomas & Associates, Inc.
185 (all): Richard Cardwell, cour. Cardwell/Thomas & Associates, Inc.
186 (top): David Jennings/*New York Times* Pictures; **(bottom):** Fred R. Conrad/*New York Times* Pictures.
187 (all): © Steve Rosenthal, cour. Graham Gund Architects.
189 (top): cour. Historic Seattle and Stickney & Murphy, Architects; **(bottom):** Tom Gohrke, cour. Stickney & Murphy, Architects.
191: © Phokion Karas, cour. Notter Finegold & Alexander Inc.

Page 192: © Steve Rosenthal, cour. Notter Finegold & Alexander Inc.
194: © Mark C. Darley, cour. Aaron Green Companies.
194-195: Jack Pottle/ESTO, cour. Aaron Green Companies.
196: cour. Ford, Powell & Carson.
198: © 1987 Philip Langdon.
199 (both): cour. Graham Gund Architects.
201: © Steve Rosenthal, cour. Graham Gund Architects.
202, 203: Lawrence W. Speck, cour. Lawrence W. Speck Associates Inc., Architects.
205 (top): cour. Moore Ruble Yudell; **(bottom left and right):** Henry Bowles, cour. Moore Ruble Yudell.
206-207: Cervin Robinson, cour. Centerbrook.
209: © Steve Rosenthal, cour. Graham Gund Architects.
210: Greg Hursley, cour. Hal Box, Architect.
211: © Steve Rosenthal, cour. Graham Gund Architects.
212: Rob Quigley.
213 (top): Rob Quigley; **(bottom):** cour. Rob Wellington Quigley, A.I.A.
214: Rob Quigley.
216, 217: © 1987 Philip Langdon.
218 (top): Rick Gardner, cour. Barnstone Architects, Houston, TX; **(bottom):** cour. Barnstone Architects, Houston, TX.
219: © 1987 Philip Langdon.
220-221, 222, 223: Rick Gardner, cour. Barnstone Architects, Houston, TX.
224 (both): Tom Bernard, cour. Venturi, Rauch and Scott Brown.
225: cour. Venturi, Rauch and Scott Brown.
226, 227: cour. Zane Yost & Associates, Inc.
229, 230-231: cour. Harry Weese & Associates.
232, 234-235, 236, 236-237: Mick Hales, cour. Orr & Taylor.
238-239: © 1985 Robert Reck, cour. Bart Prince Architect.
240 (top): Martin F.M. Grummer, cour. Bart Prince Architect; **(bottom):** © 1985 Robert Reck, cour. Bart Prince Architect.
241: cour. Bart Prince Architect.
242, 243 (both), 245: © 1985 Robert Reck, cour. Bart Prince Architect.
246-247: Charles F. Johnson, cour. Bart Prince Architect.

We have endeavored to obtain the necessary permission to reprint the photographs in this volume and to provide proper acknowledgment. We welcome information on any oversight, which we will correct in subsequent printings.

Index

Pages in *italic* contain illustrations.

251

Acknowledgments

I don't know how many times I requested — and promptly received — information from the National Association of Home Builders on questions ranging from superinsulation to improvements in subdivision design to construction of "mingles" apartments. Hundreds, certainly. The builders' association, along with the American Institute of Architects and the National Trust for Historic Preservation, directed me to many innovators I otherwise would have overlooked. The staffs of the NAHB Research Foundation and the New Haven Public Library repeatedly found facts and studies I was searching for.

Thomas Fisher, Technics Editor of *Progressive Architecture,* was exceptionally generous, steering me to useful sources, reviewing a draft of Chapter Four, and answering questions at all hours. Francis T. Ventre (one of Tom Fisher's many knowledgeable acquaintances) also suggested improvements in Chapter Four. I leaned

a great deal on J. D. Ned Nisson, editor of *Energy Design Update*; Steve Bliss, senior editor of *Solar Age*; Clem Labine, editor of *The Old-House Journal*; and Ruth Eckdish Knack, senior editor of *Planning.* I appreciate the cooperation of the individuals and firms mentioned in the text and the assistance of many others, only a few of whom can be named here: Mike Bell, John S. Chaney, Michael J. Crosbie, Paul A. Knights, Ralph Knowles, Bob McCarroll, Janet McCorison, Claire Cooper Marcus, Barry M. Moore, Steve Moore, Frank Palen, Sarah Peskin, Daniel V. Scully, Douglas Sydnor, Doug Taber, Melanie Taylor, Stephen Verderber, and Bernard M. Wharton. Thanks to my editor, Roy Finamore, and the photo editors, Amla Sanghvi and Sarah Longacre, for guiding this project smoothly to completion.

Most of all, I am grateful to my wife, Maryann D. Langdon, who made the many sacrifices that made this book possible.

Composed in Times Roman by Arkotype Inc., New York, New York

Printed and bound by Toppan Printing Co., Ltd., Tokyo, Japan